# FINANCIAL SHA

## UNCOVERING THE UNCONSCIOUS PATTERNS HOLDING YOU BACK FROM WEALTH

JOSEPHINE EBEREONWU

# Table of Contents

# Introduction

In the intricate dance of life, money often plays a leading role, dictating the rhythm and pace at which we move. Yet, for many, the path to financial abundance feels elusive, shrouded in mystery and shadowed by unseen forces that seem to hold them back. "Financial Shadows: Uncovering the Unconscious Patterns Holding You Back from Wealth" invites readers to step into the light and explore the hidden dimensions of their financial landscape.

Within the pages of this transformative book lies an exploration of the subconscious mind, the silent architect of our financial realities. It delves into the depths of the beliefs, fears, and assumptions ingrained from childhood, which subtly influence our decisions and shape our economic outcomes. These invisible scripts, often inherited from family, culture, or past experiences, govern our interactions with money in ways we might not consciously recognize.

The essence of "Financial Shadows" is not merely to shed light on these ingrained patterns but to offer practical tools and strategies to rewrite them. It challenges the reader to question long-held beliefs about wealth and scarcity, encouraging a shift in mindset that paves the way for new financial possibilities. Through a blend of psychological insights and actionable advice, the book serves as a guide to dismantling the barriers that stand between individuals and their financial goals.

As readers delve deeper, they will encounter stories of individuals who have successfully navigated their financial shadows, emerging with newfound clarity and empowerment. These narratives, coupled with thought-provoking exercises and reflections, provide a roadmap for personal and financial transformation.

"Financial Shadows" is more than a financial guide; it is an invitation to a profound inner journey. It calls upon readers to confront their financial fears, acknowledge their hidden patterns, and embrace the possibility of wealth as a natural extension of a balanced and fulfilled life. With each chapter, the book seeks to illuminate the shadows that obscure financial potential, ultimately leading to a life of abundance and freedom.

This book is an essential companion for anyone ready to unearth the unconscious patterns that have held them back and to step confidently into a future of financial empowerment.

# Chapter 1: The Illusion of Wealth

## *Gleaming Facades*

In the heart of the bustling city, where skyscrapers soared to brush the clouds, the financial district stood as a testament to human ambition and ingenuity. The early morning sun cast its golden glow over the polished glass surfaces of towering buildings, each reflecting the promise of prosperity and success. The streets below, lined with meticulously maintained trees, echoed with the steady rhythm of footsteps and the hum of anticipation.

As the day unfolded, the district revealed itself as a hive of activity. Men and women, clad in tailored suits and carrying sleek briefcases, navigated the labyrinth of streets with purpose. Their faces were masks of determination, eyes hidden behind the mirrored lenses of designer sunglasses. The air was thick with the scent of freshly brewed coffee and the faint tang of exhaust from the endless parade of taxis and luxury cars.

The architecture of the district was a symphony of steel and glass, each building a monument to modern design. Lobbies were grandiose, with marbled floors that gleamed under the soft glow of chandelier light. Walls were adorned with abstract art, each piece chosen to reflect the cutting-edge ethos of its inhabitants. Elevators, swift and silent, ferried occupants to their destinations, their doors whispering shut with hushed efficiency.

Within these edifices of commerce, the heartbeat of the financial world pulsed. Trading floors buzzed with the frenetic energy of brokers and traders, their voices rising in a cacophony of deals and negotiations. Screens flickered with streams of data, numbers, and graphs painting an ever-changing picture of global markets. Offices were sanctuaries of focus, where decisions were made that could sway the tides of fortune.

Yet, beneath the polished veneer, lay a complex web of ambition and rivalry. The pursuit of success was relentless, a race where only the swiftest and shrewdest survived. Alliances were forged and broken with the same speed as financial transactions; trust was a currency as volatile as the stock market itself.

Outside, the city continued its relentless march forward. Sidewalks teemed with people, each a player in the grand theater of commerce. Street vendors called out, their voices rising above the din of the city, offering sustenance to the weary and the rushed. The cacophony of life was a constant reminder that the world beyond the glass walls was as vibrant and unpredictable as the markets themselves.

As the sun dipped below the horizon, the district transformed once more. Lights flickered on, illuminating the buildings in a soft glow that mirrored the stars above. The city, never truly at rest, continued its dance of shadows and light, a testament to the ceaseless ebb and flow of the financial tides.

In this world of gleaming facades, the lines between reality and aspiration blurred, leaving in their wake a landscape that was both awe-inspiring and enigmatic. It was a place where dreams were built and shattered, where fortunes were made and lost, all beneath the watchful gaze of the city that never slept.

## Invisible Threads

In the dimly lit rooms of the financial district, where skyscrapers cast long shadows over bustling streets, unseen forces weave their intricate webs. The air is thick with the scent of ambition, mingling with the subtle aroma of freshly brewed coffee and the faint whiff of polished leather. Here, in this urban jungle, the pulse of the economy beats with a steady, relentless rhythm.

The city, a living organism, thrives on the invisible threads that connect its myriad parts. These threads, spun from whispers in boardrooms and the silent hum of servers in climate-controlled data centers, hold together the delicate tapestry of finance. They are the unseen hands that guide the flow of capital, the silent architects behind the rise and fall of fortunes.

In this world, numbers dance across screens in an endless ballet, their movements choreographed by unseen maestros. Algorithms, complex and unfathomable to the untrained eye, execute trades with precision, their decisions rooted in patterns discernible only to those who know where to look. The traders, mere conduits for these digital whispers, watch as fortunes are made and lost in the blink of an eye.

Beyond the glass facades of the financial towers, where sunlight struggles to penetrate, lies a realm of hushed conversations and knowing glances. Here, deals are brokered over power lunches, and alliances are forged in the quiet corners of exclusive clubs. The language spoken is one of leverage and liquidity, where every word carries weight and every gesture is loaded with meaning.

A certain kind of magic exists in the way these threads bind people and institutions, creating a complex network of influence and opportunity. It is a magic born of trust and trepidation, where the balance between risk and reward is constantly renegotiated. In this delicate dance, the players are both puppets and puppeteers, their fates intertwined in ways they cannot always perceive.

The city streets, bustling with life, are the arteries through which the lifeblood of commerce flows. Each block, each intersection, is a node in the vast network, connected by the invisible threads of commerce and trade. The people who traverse these streets, from the high-powered executives to the street vendors peddling their wares, are all part of the same intricate system.

In the quiet moments, when the city pauses to catch its breath, one can almost sense the hum of these invisible threads, vibrating with the energy of countless transactions. It is a symphony of ambition and aspiration, a testament to the power of human ingenuity and the relentless pursuit of progress.

Yet, beneath the surface, these threads can fray and unravel, leaving chaos in their wake. The fragility of the system is masked by its apparent strength, a reminder that even the most robust structures can be brought down by a single, unseen flaw. In this world of financial shadows, where certainty is an illusion, the only constant is change, and the only truth is that nothing is ever truly as it seems.

## Echoes of Prosperity

The city hummed with an undercurrent of affluence, a vibrant symphony of commerce and ambition that echoed through its bustling streets and gleaming skyscrapers. From the early morning light cascading over the glass facades to the soft glow of streetlights at dusk, the city seemed to breathe prosperity.

In the heart of the metropolis, the financial district stood as a testament to the power of wealth and the unyielding pursuit of success. Towering edifices, crafted from steel and glass, reached towards the sky, reflecting the ambitions of those who toiled within. The air was thick with the scent of freshly brewed coffee, mingling with the sharp, metallic tang of industry, as professionals clad in tailored suits navigated the labyrinth of opportunity.

The sidewalks were a tapestry of hurried footsteps, each one a beat in the relentless rhythm of commerce. Here, deals were struck with the precision of a master craftsman, each contract a delicate ballet of negotiation and strategy. The clatter of keyboards and the soft murmur of voices filled the air, a constant reminder of the ceaseless drive that fueled the city's economy.

Inside the offices, sunlight filtered through floor-to-ceiling windows, casting intricate patterns on polished wooden floors and leather-bound chairs. Conference rooms buzzed with energy, the air charged with the intensity of innovation and the promise of growth.

The walls, adorned with art that whispered tales of past triumphs, bore silent witness to the unfolding drama of financial conquest.

Yet, beneath the veneer of prosperity, shadows lingered. In the quiet moments when the city paused to catch its breath, whispers of uncertainty echoed through the corridors. The delicate balance of success and failure teetered on a knife's edge, swayed by the unseen forces of market fluctuations and global events.

Amidst the grandeur, there were those whose eyes were perpetually cast towards the horizon, seeking the next wave of opportunity. Their minds were a cacophony of numbers and projections, visions of futures yet to be realized. For them, each day was a new canvas, awaiting the strokes of daring ventures and calculated risks.

As the sun dipped below the skyline, painting the city in hues of gold and crimson, the streets began to empty, leaving behind the faint echoes of a day filled with ambition. The city, ever resilient, stood as a monument to the enduring spirit of human endeavor.

In the stillness of the evening, the echoes of prosperity lingered, a testament to the dreams and aspirations that drove the heart of the metropolis. The city, with its dazzling facade and hidden depths, continued its dance with destiny, forever entwined in the delicate waltz of fortune and fate. Here, in the shadows of financial success, the story of prosperity unfolded, a narrative as old as time itself, yet ever new in its telling.

## The Unseen Costs

In the dimly lit corners of our financial world, there exist costs that many overlook, hidden beneath the surface like the shadowy undercurrents of a vast ocean. These costs, though unseen, ripple through the lives of individuals and societies alike, weaving a complex tapestry of consequences that are often felt but rarely acknowledged.

Consider the emotional toll exacted by financial stress, a silent burden that weighs heavily on the shoulders of many. This stress does not announce itself with the blaring sirens of an immediate crisis, but rather creeps in quietly, manifesting as anxiety, sleepless nights, and strained relationships. It is the gnawing worry that eats away at one's peace of mind, leaving behind a trail of mental and physical health issues that can persist for years. As the mind becomes consumed with financial concerns, the ability to focus on work, family, and self-care diminishes, creating a vicious cycle that is difficult to break.

Beyond the individual, communities too bear the brunt of these hidden costs. When financial instability becomes a common thread, it can unravel the social fabric, leading to increased crime rates, diminished trust, and a sense of hopelessness. The lack of economic opportunities often fuels disillusionment, causing talent to wither in the shadows or migrate in search of greener pastures. This migration, in turn, depletes communities of their most valuable resource—people—leaving behind hollowed-out towns and cities struggling to maintain their vibrancy.

The environmental cost is another shadow that looms large yet remains largely unaccounted for. In the relentless pursuit of profit, the exploitation of natural resources often proceeds unchecked, leading to the degradation of ecosystems and the loss of biodiversity. The financial gains reaped from such ventures are often short-lived, while the damage left in their wake endures for generations. The cost of restoring these ecosystems, if attempted at all, is often prohibitive, leaving future generations to inherit a diminished world.

Moreover, the unseen costs extend into the realm of societal inequality. As wealth becomes concentrated in the hands of a few, the gap between the rich and poor widens, creating a chasm that is difficult to bridge. This disparity breeds resentment and fuels social unrest, as those left behind struggle to access basic necessities like education, healthcare, and housing. The cost of inequality is not just measured in economic terms but also in the loss of potential, as countless individuals are denied the opportunity to contribute meaningfully to society.

In the corporate world, the obsession with short-term gains often blinds decision-makers to the long-term implications of their actions. The pressure to deliver immediate results to shareholders can lead to cost-cutting measures that undermine employee well-being, product quality, and ethical standards. The fallout from such decisions can be catastrophic, eroding consumer trust and damaging reputations that took years to build.

The unseen costs are woven into the very fabric of our financial systems, often lurking just beneath the surface, waiting to emerge when least expected. They serve as a reminder that every financial decision carries with it a web of consequences, both seen and unseen, that must be carefully considered. Only by acknowledging and addressing these hidden costs can we hope to build a more equitable and sustainable future.

# Chapter 2: The Maze of Investments

## *Alluring Entrances*

In the dimly lit corridors of the financial world, where numbers dance like shadows on the walls, there exists an enigmatic allure. As one steps into this realm, the very air seems to hum with the promise of untold wealth and the subtle whispers of risks lurking in the corners. The atmosphere is thick with anticipation, a tantalizing blend of opportunity and uncertainty that calls to those who dare to venture into its depths.

The grand entrance to this world is a spectacle to behold. Towering skyscrapers, their glass facades gleaming under the sun, stand as silent sentinels guarding the secrets within. Each building, a monument to ambition and human endeavor, exudes a sense of power and authority. The bustling streets below teem with life, a vibrant tapestry of hurried footsteps and the ceaseless chatter of commerce.

Inside, the scene unfolds with an almost theatrical flair. Marble floors echo with the click of expensive heels, while the air is perfumed with the scent of polished wood and freshly printed documents. The architecture, a blend of modern minimalism and classical opulence, reflects the dual nature of finance itself, rooted in tradition yet ever-evolving.

Against this backdrop, figures move with purpose and precision, each one a player in the intricate ballet of the markets. Traders, analysts, and executives glide through the space, their eyes alight with the fire of ambition. They are the architects of dreams, sculpting fortunes from the raw materials of data and speculation.

The hum of technology is a constant companion, the soft whir of computers and the gentle glow of screens casting a futuristic sheen over the proceedings. Here, information is king, and the flow of data is relentless. Charts flicker with vibrant colors, each line and curve telling its own story of potential gain or devastating loss.

Conversations fill the air, a symphony of jargon and numbers that to the uninitiated might seem like an impenetrable code. But for those within the circle, it is a language of its own, a dialect of profit and prediction. Deals are struck with the precision of a surgeon's scalpel, each decision a calculated risk weighed against the scales of reward.

Yet, amidst the allure and the promise, there is an underlying tension, a reminder that the stakes in this game are high. The specter of failure looms ever-present, a shadow that trails behind even the most successful. It is this very tension that adds to the allure, the thrill of the gamble, the possibility of triumph against the odds.

In this world, the boundaries between reality and illusion blur, creating a landscape where fortunes can be made and lost in the blink of an eye. It is a place of both wonder and trepidation, where the courageous find their mettle tested and the cautious tread carefully. Here, in this captivating dance of light and shadow, the journey begins, and the allure of the entrances never fades.

## Hidden Paths

In the dimly lit corner of the bustling financial district, where shadows crept along the cobblestone streets, a world unseen by the ordinary eye thrived. It was a realm where whispered secrets and coded messages passed hands under the guise of legitimate transactions, a place where fortunes were both made and lost in the blink of an eye.

The labyrinthine alleys crisscrossing this clandestine world held stories etched in the very bricks that lined them. Each turn and twist seemed to unravel a new chapter in the lives of those who navigated its hidden paths. The air was thick with anticipation, as if the city itself was holding its breath, waiting for the next move in a game of invisible chess.

In the heart of this enigmatic web, a figure moved with a blend of purpose and caution. His footsteps were soft yet deliberate, echoing faintly in the silence that enveloped him. Clad in a tailored suit that spoke of both wealth and discretion, he blended seamlessly into the background, a shadow among shadows.

Every step he took was calculated, a dance of precision across the uneven terrain of the financial underworld. His eyes, sharp and discerning, scanned the surroundings with an acuity honed by years of navigating the delicate balance between risk and reward. He was a man who understood the power of information, and in this hidden realm, knowledge was the currency that held the greatest value.

As the figure approached a nondescript building, its facade unremarkable to the casual observer, he paused momentarily, gauging the subtle cues that lay hidden in the everyday. The flicker of a streetlamp, the rustle of leaves in an unseen breeze, the distant hum of the city, all spoke to him in a language only the initiated could decipher.

Inside, the atmosphere was one of subdued elegance, the muted glow of chandeliers casting a warm light over polished surfaces and plush furnishings. Here, in this sanctuary from the bustling world outside, deals were struck and alliances forged, all beneath the veneer of civility.

The figure moved with the ease of familiarity, acknowledging nods from those who recognized him, their expressions a blend of respect and wariness. He was both an ally and a competitor, a figure whose presence demanded attention and caution in equal measure.

In this hidden world, the paths were many and varied, each leading to possibilities both perilous and promising. It was a place where the line between success and ruin was as thin as a whisper, where the shadows held secrets that could change the course of a life.

And so, amidst the flickering shadows and the dance of light, the figure continued his journey, a silent navigator of the hidden paths that wove through the financial shadows. In this world of whispers and shadows, he thrived, a master of the unseen, carving his path through the enigmatic labyrinth of the financial underworld.

## The Labyrinth's Core

Beneath the towering facade of the financial district, where skyscrapers glisten like sentinels of wealth, lies a tangled web of corridors unseen by the public eye. Here, in the heart of this concrete jungle, lies the true essence of the financial world—a labyrinth where shadows dance and secrets are whispered.

The air is thick with the scent of polished marble and the faint hum of distant conversations. Each step echoes ominously against the cold, hard floors as if the very building is alive, listening to every footfall. Dim lights flicker above, casting a muted glow that barely illuminates the path ahead, leaving corners steeped in mystery.

Walls lined with abstract art and cryptic symbols give the impression of an exclusive gallery, a testament to the opulence that thrives in this hidden realm. Ornate doors, each more imposing than the last, guard the entrances to rooms where decisions of global consequence are made. Behind these portals, the movers and shakers of the financial world gather, their discussions a symphony of hushed tones and calculated pauses.

In this core, time seems to flow differently. The ticking of clocks is drowned by the constant ticking of stock tickers, a relentless reminder of the ever-changing landscape of fortune. Here, deals are struck with the precision of a master craftsman, each word weighed, each gesture scrutinized. There is an art to the negotiations, a dance of power cloaked in civility.

The labyrinth's core is a place of paradoxes, where ambition and trepidation walk hand in hand. The walls seem to pulse with the energy of those who pass through, absorbing the ambition and fear that fuel this world. It is a place where dreams are forged and shattered in equal measure, where the pursuit of wealth is both a noble quest and a perilous journey.

Yet, for all its grandeur, there is a haunting hollowness to this place. The absence of natural light casts a pallor over everything, a reminder that beneath the glittering surface lies a world that thrives in shadows. The labyrinth is a living entity, a creature of complexity and contradiction, where the lines between right and wrong blur, and morality is a malleable concept.

As one delves deeper into this core, the weight of its history becomes apparent. The walls bear silent witness to the triumphs and failures of those who have passed through, their stories etched invisibly into the very fabric of this place. It is a testament to the enduring nature of human ambition, a monument to the relentless pursuit of power.

Here, in the labyrinth's core, the true nature of the financial world is laid bare. It is a place of shadows and light, where the pursuit of wealth is both a blessing and a curse. And as one navigates this complex maze, the realization dawns that the labyrinth is not merely a physical space but a reflection of the human condition—a reminder that in the world of finance, the greatest challenges lie not in the numbers but in the shadows that dance just beyond the reach of light.

## Exits and Entrances

The world of finance is akin to a grand theater, where exits and entrances define the rhythm of the narrative. Each movement is choreographed with precision, every actor on this stage of numbers and negotiations playing their part to perfection. As the curtain rises, the spotlight shifts to the bustling corridors of the stock exchange. Here, the air is thick with anticipation, a palpable energy that pulses through the veins of traders and investors alike.

In this arena, exits are not merely departures; they are strategic retreats, orchestrated with the finesse of a maestro conducting a symphony. The decision to withdraw from a position is seldom taken lightly. It is a calculated move, driven by a confluence of market signals, risk assessments, and the ever-present whisper of intuition. As traders navigate this complex web of data and emotion, they become attuned to the subtle cues that herald an impending shift. A dip in market sentiment, a fluctuation in currency values, or a sudden geopolitical tremor can all serve as harbingers of change.

Yet, while exits may signify a closing chapter, they also pave the way for new beginnings. The entrance into a fresh opportunity is infused with the thrill of the unknown. It is a dance of daring and deliberation, where the allure of potential gains is balanced against the specter of unforeseen pitfalls. In these moments, the financial world reveals its dual nature, a realm where fortune favors the bold yet rewards the prudent.

The art of entrance lies in the ability to discern value where others see only volatility. It requires a keen eye and an unwavering resolve, a willingness to delve into the labyrinthine depths of market analysis. The successful investor is one who can sift through the noise, identifying trends that others overlook and seizing opportunities that lie hidden beneath the surface. These entrances are marked by a quiet confidence, a conviction borne of meticulous research and an acute awareness of the broader economic landscape.

As the cycle of exits and entrances unfolds, the financial shadows lengthen and retract, casting their influence over the fortunes of many. This perpetual dance is both a test of endurance and a testament to the resilience of those who participate in it. For in this world, each exit and entrance is a step in an ongoing journey, a reminder that the path to prosperity is seldom linear.

The interplay between departure and arrival is a delicate balance, a testament to the intricate dynamics that define the financial markets. It is a world where timing is everything, and the ability to adapt is paramount. As traders and investors navigate this ever-changing landscape, they are guided by a singular truth: that in the realm of finance, exits and entrances are not merely points of transition, but moments of transformation, where the seeds of future success are sown amid the shadows of uncertainty.

In this theater of financial endeavors, the audience watches with bated breath, knowing that the next act is always moments away, and with it, the promise of new exits and entrances that will shape the fortunes of those who dare to play their part.

# Chapter 3: Debt's Whisper

## *Enticing Promises*

As the sun dipped below the horizon, casting a warm glow over the bustling city, the financial district came alive with a hum of activity. Glass skyscrapers reflected the fiery hues of dusk, a deceptive beauty that masked the intricate web of ambition and intrigue within. Here, in the labyrinth of wealth and power, fleeting whispers of fortune danced on the lips of the hopeful.

Amidst the towering giants of finance, a quaint, almost forgotten alley wound its way through the shadows. This narrow passage, cobbled and worn, seemed an unlikely avenue for success. Yet, it was here that the most enticing promises were woven, spun from the threads of dreams and desperation.

In a dimly lit office at the alley's end, the air was thick with anticipation. Papers lay strewn across a mahogany desk, their edges curling like secrets eager to escape. The room was filled with the scent of aged leather and polished wood, a testament to deals made and lost. A single lamp illuminated the face of its occupant, casting sharp shadows that danced across the walls like specters of the past.

He was a man of indeterminate age, his features marked by the passage of time yet softened by an air of charisma. His eyes, sharp and calculating, flickered with the promise of untold wealth. With a practiced hand, he sifted through the papers, each one a potential key to unlocking a treasure trove of opportunity.

Outside, the city pulsed with life, unaware of the quiet machinations within. People hurried past, their footsteps a rhythmic beat against the cobblestones. Some were drawn to the alley by the allure of prosperity, others by the faint hope of escaping the shadows of their own making.

The man in the office understood the power of promises. He knew they were not mere words but potent spells capable of weaving dreams into reality. Yet, he also understood their double-edged nature, for promises could just as easily unravel, leaving nothing but echoes of what might have been.

As the evening deepened, the room filled with a hushed expectancy. The man leaned back in his chair, surveying the chaos of papers with a satisfied smile. Each document represented a story waiting to be told, a life poised on the brink of transformation.

The city outside continued its relentless pace, its inhabitants oblivious to the delicate dance of fate occurring within those walls. For in that dimly lit office, amidst the enticing promises and whispered dreams, the financial shadows loomed large, casting their influence far beyond the alley's confines.

Here, fortunes were made and lost, not in the glaring spotlight of the boardroom but in the quiet corners where ambition and desperation met. As the night wore on, the man remained a solitary figure, a master of the shadows, weaving his web with the deftness of a seasoned artisan.

In the world of finance, nothing was ever as it seemed. Promises, though enticing, were but the first step into a realm where shadows held sway, and the pursuit of prosperity was a journey fraught with peril and possibility.

## Subtle Shackles

The morning sun cast a gentle glow through the window, illuminating the room with a deceptive warmth that belied the cold steel grip of financial constraints that lay hidden beneath the surface. With each passing day, these invisible chains tightened, weaving themselves into the fabric of daily life, whispering promises of security while entangling aspirations in their unyielding grip.

In the bustling city, where skyscrapers reached for the heavens and neon signs blinked tirelessly into the night, the rhythm of existence was dictated by the tick of the clock and the hum of commerce. Each individual, a cog in the vast machine, moved with purpose, their steps synchronized to the beat of economic necessity. Yet, beneath the polished exterior of prosperity, a labyrinth of obligations twisted and turned, drawing its captives deeper into its intricate web.

The allure of financial freedom dangled like a distant mirage, tantalizing and elusive. It was the promise of a life unencumbered by the weight of debt, a life where dreams were not deferred but realized. Yet, with every swipe of a card or click of a button, the shackles tightened, each transaction a link in the chain that bound them. The allure of the new, the shiny, the "must-have" was a siren's call that echoed through the corridors of desire, drowning out the quiet pleas of prudence.

In the heart of this financial maze, the subtlety of the shackles was their greatest strength. They were not forged of iron or steel but of promises and expectations, of societal norms and personal ambitions. They whispered in soothing tones, convincing their bearers that the path they trod was the only one worth walking. They painted visions of success, stability, of happiness, yet left behind the bitter aftertaste of compromise and sacrifice.

The weight of these shackles bore down on shoulders already burdened by the weight of responsibility. The dreams of the past, once vibrant and full of hope, faded into shadows, obscured by the pressing demands of the present. Yet, amid the shadows, flickers of resilience remained. The human spirit, though tested, was not easily extinguished. It searched for light, for cracks in the veneer of inevitability through which it could breathe free.

In the quiet moments, when the world slowed and the noise of commerce faded to a distant hum, the truth of these shackles became apparent. They were not unbreakable, not insurmountable. They were as much a product of the mind as they were of the world outside. To cast them off required courage, a willingness to confront the shadows and step into the light of possibility.

In this balance between constraint and freedom, between the known and the unknown, lay the true challenge. It was a dance of choices, a negotiation with the self, a journey through the shadows towards a horizon yet unseen. And in that journey, the subtle shackles, once heavy and confining, could become the stepping stones to a future where the weight of financial shadows no longer held sway.

## The Burdened Mind

The streets echoed with the distant hum of the city, a constant reminder of the ceaseless activity that thrived within its concrete veins. Yet, amidst this vibrant tapestry, there existed a world cloaked in shadows, where the mind was both architect and prisoner of its own financial labyrinth.

In the dim glow of an overhead light, Elijah sat hunched over a cluttered desk, stacks of papers and ledgers forming precarious towers around him. Each document bore the weight of decisions past, a testament to choices made in moments of both clarity and desperation. His fingers traced the edges of a crumpled receipt, a relic of a transaction long forgotten, yet its significance lingered like a specter in his thoughts.

The room was silent, save for the rhythmic ticking of an old clock on the mantelpiece, its hands marching forward with an unrelenting precision. Time, a relentless adversary, seemed to mock him with each passing second. Elijah's mind wandered through the corridors of his past, each turn revealing a different facet of his financial odyssey. From the naive optimism of youthful ambition to the cautious pragmatism that now governed his every move, his journey had been one of both growth and burden.

The weight of expectation hung heavily on his shoulders, an invisible shroud that intertwined with the very fabric of his being. It was a burden born not just of external pressures, but of an internal dialogue that played on a loop, questioning every choice, every risk, every missed opportunity. The mind, he realized, was a battlefield, and the struggle for peace was often waged in silence.

In moments of quiet reflection, Elijah pondered the nature of wealth and the shadows it cast. Was it a tool of liberation, or a chain that bound its possessor? The question lingered, unanswered, as he sifted through the detritus of financial endeavors, searching for clarity amid the chaos. Each ledger told a story, a narrative woven with threads of aspiration and regret, success and failure.

The allure of prosperity, once a beacon guiding his ambitions, now seemed a distant star, its light obscured by the fog of uncertainty. Yet, within this fog, Elijah found a peculiar solace. The burdened mind, he mused, was not a curse but a crucible, forging resilience in the fires of adversity. It was a testament to the human spirit's capacity to endure, to adapt, and to find meaning in the midst of turmoil.

As the night wore on, the city outside slumbered beneath a blanket of darkness, its pulse slowing to a gentle rhythm. Elijah remained at his desk, a solitary figure illuminated by the soft glow of a single lamp. In that moment, he understood that the shadows he navigated were not just financial but existential, a reflection of the complex interplay between desire, fear, and the relentless pursuit of balance.

The burdened mind, he concluded, was both a challenge and a companion, an integral part of the journey that lay ahead. And as he closed his eyes, he embraced the shadows, knowing that within them lay the seeds of understanding, waiting to be nurtured under the light of a new dawn.

## Breaking Free

The room was dimly lit, casting long shadows across the faded carpet. The walls, once pristine white, now bore the weight of years, their surfaces adorned with remnants of past tenants—pencil marks from growth charts, faded photographs, and the occasional patch of peeling paint. A single window, draped with heavy curtains, let in a sliver of moonlight that danced across the room like a ghostly specter.

In the center of this scene sat a worn leather-bound journal, its pages filled with the musings of a mind suffocated by financial constraints. Each word penned on those yellowed pages was a testament to the struggle between dreams and the harsh reality of economic limitations. The journal was a sanctuary, a place where thoughts flowed freely, unencumbered by the weight of unpaid bills and looming debts.

As the clock ticked away the seconds, a sense of urgency filled the air. The desire to break free from the chains of financial shadows grew stronger with each passing moment. The room, though familiar and comforting in its own way, felt like a cage. The walls seemed to close in, and the ceiling loomed lower, as if conspiring to keep its occupant trapped in a cycle of fiscal despair.

Outside, the world moved on, oblivious to the silent battle waged within those four walls. The hum of distant traffic was a constant reminder of life beyond the confines of the room. It was a world full of opportunities and possibilities, but one that seemed always just out of reach.

Yet, in the stillness of that moment, a flicker of hope emerged. It was a small, fragile thing, like a flame struggling to survive against a gust of wind. But it was there, and it was enough. The realization that change was possible, that the shadows could be dispelled, filled the room with a warmth that had long been absent.

With newfound determination, the journal was opened once more. The pen glided across the page, leaving behind a trail of ink that spoke of a future unburdened by financial woes. Plans were drafted, strategies outlined, each stroke of the pen a step closer to liberation.

The act of writing was cathartic, a release of pent-up frustration and fear. It was a declaration of intent, a vow to no longer be held captive by the constraints of monetary insufficiency. The room, though unchanged in its appearance, now felt different. It was no longer a prison but a cocoon, a place of transformation where dreams could be nurtured until they were ready to take flight.

As the final words were penned, the journal was closed with a sense of satisfaction. The journey ahead was daunting, filled with challenges and uncertainties, but the first step had been taken. The shadows, while still present, seemed less intimidating, their hold on the future weakening with each passing moment.

The room, once a symbol of entrapment, now resonated with the promise of change. The moonlight, no longer a mere sliver, poured in through the window, illuminating the path forward. It was a path that led away from the shadows, towards a horizon painted with the colors of hope and freedom.

# Chapter 4: The Credit Mirage

## Mirrored Halls

The corridors stretched infinitely, a labyrinth of reflection and deception, where every step echoed the whispers of ambition and the silent screams of lost dreams. The walls, clad in polished glass, mirrored not just the physical form but the very essence of those who dared to walk their lengths. Here, in these mirrored halls, reality blurred with illusion, a fitting metaphor for the world of finance, where shadows often masquerade as truths.

The air was thick with an intoxicating blend of anticipation and dread, a cocktail of emotions that seeped into the very pores of those who wandered through. Each mirror told a story, not in words but in the subtle shifts of light and shadow, capturing fleeting glimpses of the inner turmoil that so often accompanied the chase for wealth. It was a place where the past collided with the present, where every decision, every triumph, and every failure was etched into the reflective surfaces.

As one moved deeper into the maze, the mirrors seemed to come alive, their surfaces rippling with the energy of countless souls who had passed before. They were silent witnesses to the dance of power and greed, capturing the moments of glory and despair with an unwavering gaze. In the reflective depths, the eyes of the onlooker met their own, a reminder of the duality that lay within. It was a place where one could not hide from themselves, where the facades carefully constructed in the outside world were stripped away, leaving only the raw, unfiltered truth.

The floors, a mosaic of marble and obsidian, resonated with the rhythmic cadence of footsteps, each step a reminder of the journey undertaken. The path was not always clear, often obscured by the dazzling reflections that played tricks on the mind. Yet, for those who dared to look beyond the surface, the mirrors offered insights, a glimpse into the intricate tapestry of choices that defined one's fate in the financial realm.

In the corners, where the light struggled to reach, shadows gathered like silent spectators, their presence a constant reminder of the risks that lurked in the periphery. Here, the line between success and failure was as thin as the glass itself, a fragile boundary that could shatter with the slightest misstep. It was a place where fortunes were made and lost, where dreams were both realized and crushed under the weight of expectation.

The mirrored halls were a sanctuary and a prison, a place of introspection and revelation. They held the promise of untold riches, yet demanded a price that few were willing to pay. In the end, it was a test of character, a crucible where the soul was laid bare, and only those with the courage to face their own reflection could hope to emerge unscathed.

In this world of reflections and shadows, one learned to navigate with caution, to tread lightly on the path of ambition. For within these halls, the greatest challenge was not the competition or the market forces, but the battle within oneself, a battle that played out in the silent dialogue between the heart and the mind, captured forever in the mirrored reflections of the soul.

## Concealed Reflections

In the dim glow of the late afternoon sun, the cityscape cast elongated shadows that seemed to stretch across the bustling streets like fingers reaching out to touch the unknown. The world of finance, much like these shadows, held secrets and mysteries within its depths, obscured from the untrained eye. It was here, amid the towering skyscrapers and the relentless pulse of commerce, that the true nature of financial shadows began to unravel—a hidden world of reflections, both literal and metaphorical.

As the sun dipped lower in the sky, its golden light danced across the glass facades of the financial district's imposing structures. Each pane, a mirror capturing and distorting the reality it reflected, offered glimpses of the lives intertwined within. The hurried steps of a broker, the furrowed brow of an analyst deep in thought, the laughter of colleagues sharing a moment of reprieve—each scene played out in the shimmering glass, a silent testament to the human stories woven into the fabric of finance.

Yet, beneath this surface of polished glass and concrete, lay the concealed reflections—the intricate patterns of decisions, risks, and strategies that shaped the financial landscape. Like an artist's brushstrokes hidden beneath layers of paint, these reflections were not immediately visible, but they defined the essence of the picture. In boardrooms and trading floors, whispers of market trends and future forecasts echoed, forming a symphony of calculated moves and cautious optimism.

The world of finance, much like an intricate dance, requires precision and a keen understanding of timing. Each decision made was a step in this complex choreography, where a misstep could result in unforeseen consequences. The concealed reflections of past choices linger, reminding those who dared to navigate these waters of the delicate balance between risk and reward.

Amid this backdrop, the individuals who inhabited this world became both creators and observers of these reflections. The seasoned investors, with their keen eyes and honed instincts, could discern the subtle shifts in the market's temperament. Their intuition, born from years of experience, allowed them to anticipate the ripples that would soon cascade through the financial ecosystem.

For the uninitiated, however, these reflections remained elusive, hidden behind a veil of complexity and jargon. The language of finance, with its acronyms and terminologies, acted as a barrier, separating the initiated from those who remained on the periphery.

But for those willing to delve deeper, to peer beyond the surface, the reflections offered a wealth of insights and opportunities.

As the last rays of sunlight faded, the city transformed into a landscape of twinkling lights, each representing a story, a decision, a reflection of the financial world. In this twilight, the true nature of financial shadows came to life, revealing both the challenges and the potential that lay within. It was a world of contrasts, where light and shadow danced in harmony, creating a tapestry of endless possibilities.

In this realm of concealed reflections, the journey was not merely about numbers and charts, but about understanding the narratives that shaped them. It was about seeing beyond the immediate, recognizing the patterns, and embracing the complexity that defined the financial shadows.

## The True Image

In the half-light of the trading floor, where numbers flicker like ghostly apparitions on a multitude of screens, the cacophony of voices and the staccato clatter of keyboards form a symphony of modern commerce. Here, amidst the hum of technology and the palpable tension of high-stakes decision-making, the true image of finance begins to reveal itself — an intricate dance between the seen and the unseen, the tangible and the ephemeral.

The room is a sea of motion, where traders move with a practiced precision, their eyes darting between screens, fingers tapping out commands as swiftly as thoughts form. The air buzzes with the electricity of anticipation, the atmosphere thick with the scent of ambition and anxiety. Each individual is a cog in a vast machine, their roles defined by the invisible lines of code and the algorithms that dictate the financial tides.

Screens flicker with rows of numbers, red and green, climbing and plummeting with the rhythm of an unpredictable heartbeat. They are the lifeblood of this world, carrying messages from distant markets, whispers of trends, and the echoes of decisions made in boardrooms far removed from

this frenetic epicenter. The traders' eyes are trained to decipher this language, to see beyond the surface into the depths of what these numbers truly mean.

In this realm, the concept of wealth is both concrete and abstract. It takes form in the graphs that chart the trajectories of fortunes made and lost, yet it remains a phantom, elusive and shifting, always just beyond the grasp of those who pursue it with relentless determination. Here, success is measured not in the currency of the tangible, but in the ability to predict the unpredictable, to ride the crest of a wave before it crashes.

The traders themselves are a study in contrasts, their faces etched with the lines of concentration, yet their eyes alight with the thrill of the chase. They are both the creators and the created, shaping the markets even as they are shaped by them, their destinies intertwined with the ebb and flow of capital. Their conversations are a rapid-fire exchange of jargon and speculation, each word a piece in the puzzle of global finance.

Above it all, the hum of computers provides a constant backdrop, a reminder of the ever-watchful presence of technology. It is both ally and adversary, a tool that provides the edge yet demands vigilance, for in this world, the margin for error is razor-thin. The traders' reliance on these machines is absolute, yet there is an unspoken understanding that beneath the digital veneer lies the true heart of the market — human instinct and emotion.

As the day wears on, the frenetic pace shows no sign of abating. The traders remain at their stations, eyes fixed on the screens, fingers poised to react to the slightest shift. In this relentless environment, the true image of finance emerges — a complex tapestry woven from the threads of innovation, intuition, and the inexorable pursuit of profit. It is a world in constant motion, where the only certainty is change, and the only constant is the drive to adapt and conquer the shadows that linger at the edges of the financial landscape.

## Shattering Illusions

In the dim, flickering light of the bustling financial district, the skyscrapers loomed like silent sentinels, each a towering monument to the dreams and ambitions of countless individuals. The streets were alive with the hum of activity, a cacophony of voices and footsteps that intertwined with the distant roar of traffic. Beneath this vibrant façade, however, lay a world of complexity and illusion, where the shadows of finance danced in intricate patterns, concealing as much as they revealed.

Amidst this labyrinthine network of power and wealth, the air was thick with an almost palpable tension, an undercurrent of uncertainty that seemed to pulse through the very veins of the city. It was a place where fortunes were made and lost in the blink of an eye, a realm where perception often held more weight than reality itself. Here, the lines between truth and deception blurred, creating a landscape where the most skilled navigators were those who could discern the difference.

On this particular day, the sun hung low in the sky, casting long, slanting shadows that stretched across the pavement like fingers of some unseen hand. The light was golden, yet it seemed to hold a certain sharpness, as if it were slicing through the illusions that had been carefully constructed over time. In this moment, the truth began to emerge, like a painting slowly revealing itself beneath layers of varnish.

As the city moved to its relentless rhythm, a sense of awakening stirred among those who dared to look beyond the surface. The financial markets, once perceived as infallible beacons of prosperity, began to show signs of vulnerability. The intricate web of investments and assets, meticulously woven over the years, appeared to tremble, its fragility exposed under the weight of scrutiny.

The whispers of impending change grew louder, echoing through the corridors of power and influence. Analysts and investors, once confident in their predictions, now found themselves questioning the very foundations upon which their beliefs had been built. The numbers and charts that had once seemed so definitive now appeared as mere shadows, flickering with uncertainty.

In this atmosphere of revelation, the players within the financial arena began to reassess their roles. The illusion of control, once so alluring, now seemed tenuous at best. It was a time of introspection, a moment to confront the truths that had long been obscured by the allure of success.

Yet, amidst this upheaval, there was a glimmer of hope. For in the shattering of illusions, there lay the potential for transformation. The landscape of finance, though fraught with challenges, held the promise of renewal. As the dust of disillusionment settled, a new clarity emerged, offering the possibility of a more transparent and equitable future.

In the end, the city continued to hum with life, its heart beating in sync with the aspirations of those who dared to dream anew. The shadows that once obscured the path now served as reminders of the lessons learned, guiding the way forward in a world where the light of truth shone just a little bit brighter.

# Chapter 5: Speculation's Dance

## *The Tempting Waltz*

The ballroom was bathed in a golden glow, a symphony of flickering chandeliers casting a luminous spell over the expectant crowd. The polished floor gleamed beneath the soft soles of leather shoes, a mirror reflecting the opulence of the evening. Gossamer drapes fluttered in the gentle breeze that whispered through the ornate windows, their delicate dance a prelude to the spectacle about to unfold.

In the center of this opulent setting, a grand piano stood, its ebony and ivory keys patiently awaiting the touch of a maestro. Soft murmurs of conversation mingled with the clinking of crystal glasses, a harmonious prelude to the evening's main event. The guests, adorned in their finest attire, moved like elegant phantoms, each step a calculated measure in the choreography of high society.

Amidst this sea of refinement, the air buzzed with anticipation. The scent of expensive perfumes mingled with the subtle aroma of freshly polished wood, creating an intoxicating blend that enveloped the senses. A hushed silence fell over the room as the first notes of a waltz floated through the air, tender and inviting.

The music, like a siren's call, beckoned the guests to the dance floor. It was a melody both captivating and mysterious, a composition that seemed to hold within it the secrets of the ages. The rhythm was steady, yet unpredictable, a heartbeat that pulsed through the room, igniting a spark in the souls of all who listened.

Couples began to move, their bodies swaying in perfect harmony with the enchanting tune. Dresses of silk and satin shimmered under the light, their colors blending into a kaleidoscope of motion. Each dancer seemed to glide effortlessly, as if the music had taken hold of their very being, guiding them through an intricate tapestry of steps.

Among the dancers, a figure stood out, his presence commanding yet understated. His eyes, dark and piercing, scanned the room with an intensity that belied the calm exterior he presented. Clad in a tailored suit that spoke of wealth and power, he moved with a grace that was both natural and practiced.

As the waltz reached its crescendo, the floor became a swirl of activity, a whirlwind of movement that seemed to defy the constraints of time. The music, now a tempest, carried the dancers to heights they had never imagined, each note a promise of something more, something beyond the ordinary.

In this moment, the world outside ceased to exist. The worries, the uncertainties, the shadows of financial turmoil that loomed just beyond the gilded walls were forgotten, if only for a fleeting instant. Here, within the embrace of the tempting waltz, there was only the music, the dance, and the promise of what might be.

As the final notes faded into silence, a collective sigh swept through the room, a reluctant return to reality. Yet, the magic lingered, a whisper of a promise that echoed in the hearts of all who had been touched by the night's enchanting spell. In the shadows of the financial world, where fortunes could be won or lost with a single step, the waltz remained a beacon of hope, a reminder of the beauty that could be found even in the most uncertain of times.

## The Unpredictable Rhythm

In the dimly lit corners of the financial world, where numbers dance in an endless waltz, the rhythm of the market pulses unpredictably. It's a symphony composed of countless variables; each note a potential tremor in the delicate balance of economic stability. The air is thick with the scent of

anticipation, a heady mix of anxiety and hope as investors, analysts, and market watchers try to decipher the melody.

The stock exchange, a grand theater of ambition and trepidation, stands as a testament to human resilience and folly. Here, the cacophony of voices rises and falls like a turbulent sea, each wave carrying with it the weight of fortunes won and lost. Traders, with eyes like hawks and nerves of steel, navigate this tempestuous landscape, their fingers poised above keyboards, ready to strike at the slightest hint of opportunity.

Amidst this orchestrated chaos, patterns emerge and dissolve like mirages on a scorching desert horizon. The market's rhythm is as volatile as the winds of change, swirling unpredictably, leaving behind a trail of uncertainty. One moment, the tempo is frenetic, a rapid-fire succession of trades and transactions that send prices soaring to dizzying heights. Next, it slows to a languid crawl, as if the market itself is catching its breath, contemplating its next move.

In the shadows of this financial ballet, algorithms hum softly, their binary whispers plotting strategies with precision and detachment. These silent sentinels of the digital age sift through mountains of data, seeking patterns invisible to the human eye. And yet, even these mechanical minds, with their cold calculations, cannot fully predict the market's whims. For in the end, the market is a reflection of human nature, a capricious creature given to fits of euphoria and despair.

Outside the exchange, in the bustling streets of the financial district, the rhythm extends its reach. The hum of conversation, the clatter of footsteps, and the distant wail of sirens form a backdrop to the unfolding drama. Here, in the heart of the city, the pulse of commerce beats steadily, a constant reminder of the market's far-reaching influence.

Everywhere, eyes are glued to screens, scanning for clues to the market's next move. Analysts pore over charts and graphs, their minds racing to connect the dots, to uncover the hidden symphony beneath the surface noise. Investors sit at the edge of their seats, their hearts synchronized to the tick of the clock, each second a reminder of the fleeting nature of opportunity.

Yet, amidst the unpredictability, there is a strange sense of order, a rhythm that, despite its capriciousness, follows its own logic. It is this paradox that draws people in, that compels them to engage with the market's dance, to become part of its story. For within the shadows of financial uncertainty lies the promise of possibility, a chance to ride the waves of fortune or to be swept away by the tides of fate. And so, the rhythm continues, an endless cycle of anticipation and resolution, played out on the grand stage of the financial world.

## *Partners in Motion*

The city was a sprawling labyrinth of opportunity, its skyline a jagged silhouette against the dusky horizon. In this concrete jungle, alliances were as vital as currency, and the savvy knew this truth all too well. As the sun dipped below the horizon, casting long shadows that stretched and twisted through the bustling streets, a unique dance of partnership unfurled beneath the neon-lit avenues.

In the heart of this metropolis, where glass towers pierced the heavens and the pulse of commerce was a constant thrum, individuals sought out kindred spirits. These were not mere casual acquaintances, but carefully chosen allies, each bringing their own unique value to the table. In this intricate web of connections, the right partnership could mean the difference between obscurity and prominence.

Here, amidst the cacophony of ambition and the whisper of whispered deals, the art of collaboration was honed to a fine edge. Relationships were cultivated with the precision of a master gardener tending to a prized bonsai, each branch and leaf meticulously shaped and nurtured. Trust, a fragile commodity in this realm of shadows, was earned through shared endeavors and mutual respect.

The city's cafes and boardrooms became the stage for these interactions, where ideas were exchanged over steaming cups of coffee or the clink of crystal glasses. Conversations flowed like rivers, meandering through topics of dreams, fears, and aspirations. These discussions were not just about profit, but about vision and the shared journey toward a common goal.

In this landscape, partnerships were forged with the understanding that each player had their own strengths and weaknesses. Some brought creativity, others strategy; some wielded influence, while others held deep wells of knowledge. The synergy created by these unions was akin to the harmonious blend of instruments in a symphony, each contributing its own unique sound to the overarching melody.

Yet, beneath the surface, the dynamics of these partnerships were complex and multifaceted. Navigating them required a keen understanding of human nature and the ability to anticipate needs and desires. It was a delicate balancing act, requiring intuition and foresight to ensure that the equilibrium was maintained.

Every successful partnership was underpinned by a foundation of shared values and aligned objectives. Like the gears of a well-oiled machine, these collaborations propelled those involved toward their individual and collective ambitions. In this environment, the true currency was not monetary, but the strength of relationships and the ability to adapt and grow together.

As the night deepened and the city lights twinkled like stars fallen to earth, the partnerships forged within its confines continued to thrive. They were the lifeblood of the city, fueling innovation and progress, driving the economy forward with relentless momentum. In this realm of financial shadows, partnerships were not just a means to an end but a testament to the power of collaboration and the boundless possibilities that could be achieved when minds and efforts converged.

Thus, the city thrived, a testament to the power of human connection, where partners in motion crafted their own destinies amidst the ever-shifting shadows of finance and ambition.

## The Final Bow

A hush fell over the crowded room, the air tinged with anticipation and the faint scent of polished wood and old paper. The dim lighting cast long shadows on the walls, echoing the very essence of the financial world—a dance between light and darkness, prosperity and loss. At the center of it all stood an imposing figure, a man who had spent decades weaving through the intricate tapestry of finance, his every move calculated, every word a carefully placed step in a complex ballet.

The room, filled with peers and protégés, seemed to hold its collective breath as he prepared to speak. The soft rustle of tailored suits and the delicate clink of glasses punctuated the silence. It was a gathering of power and influence, of whispered deals and unspoken alliances, each individual a player in the vast theatre of finance.

He cleared his throat, the sound resonating with authority, drawing every eye towards him. His presence was magnetic, commanding respect and admiration alike. The lines etched into his face told stories of battles won and lost, of markets tamed and fortunes built from the ashes of defeat. He stood poised at the pinnacle of his career, yet the weight of countless decisions bore heavily on his broad shoulders.

The words that followed were not mere rhetoric, but a legacy crafted in the crucible of experience. He spoke of the shadows that lurked in the financial world, of the unseen forces that shaped destinies and toppled empires. Each sentence was a brushstroke on a canvas, painting a vivid picture of a realm where success and failure were separated by the thinnest of margins.

He recounted tales of triumph and caution, of risks taken and rewards reaped. His voice, a deep and resonant melody, echoed through the room, captivating his audience with its cadence. The stories he shared were not just lessons but warnings, a reminder of the fickle nature of fortune and the relentless pursuit of wealth.

As he spoke, the room seemed to shrink, the walls closing in as if to contain the gravity of his words. The audience leaned forward, hanging on every syllable, their faces a tapestry of admiration and reflection. Here was a man who had seen the peaks and valleys of the financial landscape, who had danced with shadows and emerged, if not unscathed, then certainly wiser.

In the flickering candlelight, his eyes shone with a mixture of nostalgia and resolve. He spoke of the future, of the challenges that lay ahead for those daring enough to step into the fray. His words were a beacon, guiding the next generation through the murky waters of finance, urging them to learn from the past while forging their own paths.

As his speech drew to a close, a ripple of applause spread through the room, rising to a crescendo that reverberated off the walls. It was a fitting tribute to a life spent in the shadows, a final bow to a career that had shaped the very fabric of the financial world. He stood there, a solitary figure against the backdrop of history, the echoes of his journey resonating in the hearts of those who bore witness to his final act.

# Chapter 6: The Silent Market

## *Quiet Transactions*

From the heart of the bustling financial district, where skyscrapers kissed the sky and the hum of commerce never ceased, there existed an undercurrent—an invisible network of transactions that operated in shadows. This world, elusive and enigmatic, was not one of towering glass buildings or ticker tapes, but rather one of whispered agreements and unspoken understandings.

In this silent realm, the players were not the usual suspects of Wall Street but rather a cadre of individuals who thrived in the art of discretion. Their dealings were not broadcast on any public ledger, nor did they grace the headlines of financial news. Yet, their influence was profound, weaving through the fabric of global economies with a subtle touch.

The air was thick with anticipation as dusk settled over the city. In dimly lit backrooms, behind the façade of legitimate businesses, figures gathered. Their faces obscured by the shadows, their conversations barely audible above the ambient noise. Here, the currency was not just money but information—a commodity as valuable, if not more so, than gold or oil.

These transactions were orchestrated with a precision akin to a maestro leading an orchestra. Each note, a carefully calculated move, contributing to a symphony of financial maneuvering. Deals were struck with a nod or a handshake, their terms understood implicitly without the need for written contracts. Trust, in this world, was both a rare commodity and a powerful tool.

Among the participants were brokers who operated at the fringes of legality, their expertise in navigating the murky waters of financial regulation unparalleled. They were the facilitators, the connectors, bridging gaps between those who had and those who sought. Their role was crucial, for in this clandestine market, the flow of information was akin to the flow of blood—vital and life-sustaining.

Then there were the financiers, individuals or entities with vast reserves of capital, seeking investment opportunities away from the prying eyes of regulatory bodies. For them, these quiet transactions offered a playground where risk and reward danced a delicate tango, unencumbered by traditional oversight.

In this shadowy landscape, even the smallest ripple could create waves. A whisper of a deal could send shockwaves

through entire industries, altering the trajectory of markets without leaving a trace. It was a place where the lines between right and wrong blurred, and morality was often a matter of perspective.

Yet, for all its secrecy, this world was not devoid of its own code of ethics. There was an unspoken understanding, a mutual respect among its denizens. Loyalty was prized, and betrayal was met with swift retribution. It was an ecosystem in balance, where each participant knew their role and the importance of maintaining the status quo.

As the night deepened, the city continued to pulse with life, oblivious to the quiet transactions unfolding in its midst. For those involved, it was just another day in the shadows—an intricate dance of power, influence, and opportunity, played out far from the spotlight, yet with implications that reached far and wide.

## Invisible Hands

In the bustling heart of the financial district, where the pulse of commerce beats incessantly, lies an unseen force orchestrating the dance of numbers and fortunes. The air is thick with anticipation, a palpable tension that clings to the suits and ties that weave through the streets. Beneath the surface of this vibrant façade, hidden from the prying eyes of the everyday passerby, operates an enigmatic presence—an entity both feared and revered in equal measure.

The corridors of power are lined with gleaming glass towers that stretch skyward, their windows reflecting the ambitions of those within. Behind these walls, decisions are made in hushed tones, their implications rippling across global markets. Here, the invisible hands deftly maneuver, their touch as subtle as a whisper yet as powerful as a storm.

Inside these sanctuaries of finance, rooms are filled with an array of screens, each a portal to a different world of data and analytics. The ambient hum of computers is a constant, a background symphony to the frenetic activity that unfolds. Traders, analysts, and brokers move in a choreographed frenzy, their eyes flicking between screens and phones, fingers poised to execute the next big move. Amidst this chaos, the invisible hands weave their influence, guiding and shaping the ebb and flow of capital.

These hands belong to no one individual but rather to a collective—a network of minds and algorithms that transcend borders and time zones. They are the embodiment of strategy and foresight, their reach extending into every corner of the financial universe. With each transaction, they leave an indelible mark, a signature that is both intangible and undeniable.

Yet, for all their influence, these hands are shrouded in mystery. Their origins are the subject of speculation and intrigue, whispered about in the corridors of power and discussed in the shadows of boardrooms. Some say they are the legacy of ancient banking families, their roots entwined with the very fabric of modern finance. Others believe they are the product of cutting-edge technology, artificial intelligence crafted to perfection.

The allure of the invisible hands lies in their duality—both a force for good and a harbinger of potential chaos. They can stabilize a faltering market with a well-timed intervention or send shockwaves through economies with an unexpected shift. Their power is undeniable, yet their motives remain inscrutable, their actions often cloaked in secrecy.

As the sun sets over the city, casting long shadows across the streets below, the invisible hands continue their work, unseen yet ever-present. They are the silent architects of wealth and ruin, their influence felt but never fully understood. In this world of financial shadows, they remain the ultimate enigma, a testament to the complexity and unpredictability of the markets they govern.

Thus, the dance continues, a perpetual cycle of creation and destruction, guided by hands that leave no trace. The city sleeps, but the world of finance never rests, its every move dictated by forces unseen, its future shaped by the invisible hands that hold the reins of destiny.

## The Unheard Voices

In the bustling heart of the financial district, where skyscrapers cast long shadows over the crowded streets, an intricate tapestry of lives intertwines in the most unlikely of places. Beneath the polished façade of wealth and power lies a world often ignored, where the whispers of those who remain unseen echo through the corridors of influence.

In the dimly lit basement of a towering office building, a group of janitors begin their nightly routine. Their presence is as constant as the ticking clock, yet they remain invisible to the bustling world above. Their hands, worn and calloused, tell stories of resilience and survival, each fingerprint a testament to their silent contribution to the city's relentless pace.

Maria, with her gentle eyes and a voice that barely rises above the hum of the air conditioning, moves with practiced grace. Her life is a delicate balance of hope and hardship, a dance between the aspirations she holds for her children and the realities she faces daily. As she wipes the glass doors, she catches glimpses of her reflection—a fleeting reminder of her dreams that once soared high above the city skyline.

Nearby, her colleague, Jamal, hums a soulful tune, his deep voice resonating in the empty halls. Each note carries the weight of nostalgia, weaving memories of a distant homeland into the fabric of his present. His laughter, rich and infectious, fills the space, a momentary reprieve from the solitude of his work. Yet, beneath his jovial exterior lies a heart burdened by separation and longing, a silent hope for reunion with loved ones left behind.

In the corner, Mei meticulously polishes the brass handles, her movements precise and methodical. Her eyes, sharp and observant, miss nothing. She is the keeper of secrets, the guardian of stories that unfold in the quiet hours of the night. In Mei's silence, there is strength—a quiet determination to carve a path for her family amidst the cacophony of the city.

Above them, in a brightly lit conference room, the city's elite discuss numbers and strategies, shaping the futures of countless individuals with the flick of a pen. Their conversations, filled with jargon and projections, rarely acknowledge the hands that keep their world in motion. Yet, the janitors continue their work, their stories woven into the very fabric of the building, their voices a silent testament to the unseen forces that sustain the city's heartbeat.

As dawn breaks, the janitors retreat into the shadows, their presence fading as the city awakens. The streets fill with the rush of commuters, oblivious to the lives that have touched

their world in the quiet hours before sunrise. Yet, in the stillness of the early morning, the unheard voices linger, a gentle reminder of the resilience and dignity that thrive in the shadows.

In the end, the financial district is not just a monument to commerce and ambition, but a living, breathing entity powered by the dreams and determination of those who remain unseen. The unheard voices, though often overlooked, are the lifeblood of this vibrant ecosystem, their stories a poignant reminder of the interconnectedness of all who walk these city streets.

## The Sound of Silence

In the dimly lit corners of the financial world, where numbers dance silently on screens and decisions are whispered across mahogany tables, there exists a unique kind of quietude. It's a silence that hums with the tension of anticipation, the weight of unspoken words, and the delicate balance between risk and reward.

Here, in the heart of the financial shadows, where fortunes are made and lost in the blink of an eye, silence is more than the absence of sound. It is a presence, a force that shapes the decisions of those who dwell within its embrace. The clattering of keyboards and the soft rustle of paper are but echoes in this realm, overshadowed by the profound stillness that envelops every transaction.

This silence has a texture, a palpable density that fills the air like a thick fog. It's the silence of paused breaths, of eyes scanning screens with bated anticipation, of minds racing to calculate the next move. In this world, silence is a language, spoken fluently by those who understand its nuances. It is the pause before a decision, the space between a question and its answer, the moment when everything hangs in the balance.

The financial shadows are inhabited by figures who glide through this silence with the grace of seasoned dancers. Their movements are precise, their expressions unreadable, their intentions known only to themselves. They are the architects of deals, the weavers of complex webs, the stewards of invisible empires. Their currency is trust, their commodity is risk, and their ally is the soundless void that surrounds them.

In the depths of this silence, time itself seems to stretch and contract, bending to the will of those who navigate its currents. Minutes can feel like hours, and hours can vanish in an instant, swallowed by the relentless march of numbers and the inexorable pull of markets. Yet, within this temporal distortion, there is a clarity, a sharpness of focus that cuts through the haze of uncertainty.

The sound of silence in the financial shadows is punctuated by the occasional burst of noise—a phone ringing, a deal closing, a market crashing—but these are mere interruptions, fleeting ripples on the surface of a vast, still ocean. It is in the silence that the true work is done, where strategies are crafted, and futures are forged.

In this world, silence is both a refuge and a crucible. It is where the weight of responsibility is felt most acutely, where the stakes are highest, and where the rewards are most profound. It is a place where the past and the future converge, where decisions made in silence echo through time, shaping destinies and altering the course of lives.

The sound of silence in the financial shadows is a symphony of restraint, a melody of patience, a harmony of calculated risks and measured rewards. It is the sound of power wielded with precision, of influence exerted with subtlety, of ambition pursued with quiet determination. It is a sound that resonates in the hearts of those who dare to listen, who choose to step into the shadows, and who find in the silence a world of infinite possibility.

# Chapter 7: The Rise of Shadows

## *Emerging Figures*

In the labyrinthine corridors of global finance, new figures often emerge, casting long shadows over the established order. These individuals, with their unconventional strategies and unyielding ambition, redefine the contours of wealth and power. As they navigate the intricate web of markets, currencies, and commodities, their influence becomes palpable, altering the flow of capital across borders and reshaping economic landscapes.

The rise of these financial titans is not merely a tale of numbers and transactions; it is a story of visionaries who perceive opportunities where others see only obstacles. Their ascent is marked by a keen understanding of the subtle interplay between risk and reward. They operate at the cutting edge of innovation, leveraging technology and data analytics to outmaneuver traditional competitors. In doing so, they challenge the status quo, pushing the boundaries of what is deemed possible within the financial realm.

These emerging figures often possess a remarkable ability to anticipate market shifts, a skill that sets them apart in an arena where fortunes can be made or lost in the blink of an eye. With an astute awareness of global events, they deftly adjust their strategies, capitalizing on geopolitical tensions, economic reforms, and technological advancements. Their decisions are informed by a blend of intuition and empirical analysis, allowing them to stay ahead of the curve in an ever-evolving financial landscape.

In boardrooms and trading floors around the world, their influence is felt. They are the architects of complex financial instruments and the orchestrators of mergers and acquisitions that reshape entire industries. Their actions reverberate through stock exchanges and currency markets, impacting the lives of millions. As they ascend to prominence, they often attract both admiration and scrutiny, their every move dissected by analysts and commentators eager to unravel the secrets of their success.

Yet, the path to prominence for these financial luminaries is fraught with challenges. They must navigate a volatile environment where regulatory frameworks are constantly shifting, and economic uncertainties loom large. In this high- stakes game, adaptability and resilience are essential. They must remain vigilant, ever ready to pivot in response to unforeseen developments, while maintaining the strategic foresight that propelled them to the forefront of the financial world.

The emergence of these figures is not only a testament to their individual prowess but also a reflection of broader systemic changes within the global economy. As traditional barriers to entry diminish and access to information becomes more democratized, the playing field is leveled, allowing new players to challenge established financial hierarchies. In this dynamic landscape, innovation becomes the currency of success, and those who can harness its potential find themselves at the helm of transformative change.

In the shadows of high finance, these figures continue to rise, their presence a catalyst for both disruption and growth. As they chart their course through the complexities of modern finance, they leave an indelible mark on the world, shaping the future in ways that are both profound and far-reaching. Their journey is not just a testament to personal ambition but a reflection of the evolving nature of finance itself, where new possibilities emerge from the interplay of vision, innovation, and audacity.

## The Lengthening Silhouettes

As dusk settled over the sprawling metropolis, the cityscape transformed into a tableau of twinkling lights and towering structures. The skyline, a jagged line against the fading twilight, seemed to stretch and breathe, casting elongated shadows that danced across the streets below. Here, in this urban jungle, the financial district stood as a monument to human ambition, its skyscrapers reaching ever skyward, their silhouettes lengthening with the setting sun.

The streets below were a river of activity, teeming with a diverse cast of characters, each playing their part in the grand theater of commerce. Suited figures moved with purpose, their briefcases swinging in rhythm with their hurried steps. Their expressions were a study in determination, eyes focused ahead, minds already calculating the next move in the intricate game of finance. Amidst them, the occasional street vendor called out, offering coffee and newspapers, their voices a counterpoint to the hum of conversation and the distant roar of traffic.

In this world of high stakes and rapid transactions, the buildings themselves seemed alive, their glass facades reflecting the ebb and flow of the city's heartbeat. As the day transitioned into night, office lights flickered on, illuminating the interiors where figures could be seen moving like shadows, tethered to their desks by the invisible threads of responsibility and ambition.

From the lofty heights of these towers, the view was both majestic and humbling. The city unfurled below like a living organism, its streets a network of veins pulsating with the lifeblood of commerce. The financial district, with its gleaming towers and bustling atmosphere, was the nucleus, the heart from which the city's energy emanated.

Yet, as the shadows lengthened, there was an undeniable sense of introspection that settled over the scene. The city, so vibrant and alive during the day, seemed to pause, as if holding its breath in the quiet moments before nightfall. It was a time for reflection, for considering the delicate balance between ambition and contentment, between the pursuit of wealth and the simple pleasures of life.

For those who inhabited this world, the lengthening silhouettes served as a reminder of the passage of time, of the fleeting nature of success, and the ever-present shadow of uncertainty. In the quiet solitude of their offices, illuminated by the soft glow of computer screens and desk lamps, they pondered the day's events, weighing the gains and losses, both financial and personal.

Outside, the city continued its relentless march towards the future, the lengthening shadows a testament to the enduring cycle of day and night, of ambition and reflection. As the last light of day faded, the city embraced the cloak of night, its silhouette a constant, unchanging presence against the backdrop of an ever-evolving world.

In this moment, as the shadows stretched and the city slowed, there was a sense of unity, of shared purpose and collective aspiration. The financial district, with its towering structures and ceaseless activity, stood as a beacon of human endeavor, a testament to the relentless pursuit of dreams and the indomitable spirit of those who dared to chase them.

## Dancing in the Dark

The room was dimly lit, shadows stretching across the walls like whispers of forgotten secrets. The air was thick with the scent of aged paper and burnt coffee, mingling with the faint hum of fluorescent lights that flickered sporadically, casting an uneasy glow. In the heart of this muted chaos, Arthur sat hunched over his desk, a solitary figure enveloped in a cocoon of financial reports and spreadsheets that seemed to tower over him like looming sentinels.

His fingers moved deftly across the keyboard, each keystroke   a quiet rebellion against the encroaching darkness that threatened to swallow him whole. Numbers danced across the screen in an intricate ballet, a delicate balance between profit and loss that Arthur had spent years mastering. Yet, in this moment, they felt like cryptic hieroglyphs, their meaning just beyond his grasp, teasing him with their elusive truths.

The ticking of the clock on the far wall was a metronome, marking the passage of time with a relentless precision that Arthur found both comforting and oppressive. Each tick was a reminder of the decisions that lay before him, choices that would shape the fortunes of not just his company, but the lives of countless others who depended on his judgment.

As he leaned back in his chair, the leather creaking softly in protest, Arthur's mind wandered to the events that had brought him to this point. The financial world was a labyrinth, a complex tapestry woven with threads of ambition, greed, and fear. It was a dance, intricate and unforgiving, where one misstep could lead to ruin, and only those with the sharpest instincts and steadiest nerves could hope to survive.

He thought of the meetings, the negotiations carried out in hushed tones over polished mahogany tables, the deals struck in the shadows of boardrooms where the stakes were as high as the skyscrapers that surrounded them. Each encounter was a carefully choreographed performance, where every gesture, every word, was calculated to tip the scales in his favor.

Yet, despite the pressure, there was a thrill in the uncertainty, a pulse of adrenaline that coursed through his veins and kept him coming back for more. It was the allure of the unknown, the possibility of turning the tide with a single, decisive move that kept him tethered to the world of finance, even as it threatened to consume him whole.

The shadows in the room seemed to shift, taking on a life of their own as Arthur's thoughts drifted to the future. There was a delicate beauty in the chaos, a rhythm that he had come to understand and even embrace. As he stared at the screen, the numbers began to make sense once more, aligning into patterns that only he could decipher.

In the solitude of the dimly lit room, Arthur felt a quiet resolve settle over him. The dance was far from over, and as the shadows whispered their secrets, he knew that he was ready to face whatever lay ahead. With a renewed sense of purpose, he turned back to the screen, his fingers poised to continue the dance, to navigate the shadows and emerge into the light once more.

# The Light Beyond

In the heart of a sprawling metropolis, where the cacophony of commerce and the hum of finance create an ever-present symphony, there exists a realm often overshadowed by the towering skyscrapers and bustling trading floors. This is the domain where the intrepid few dare to seek what lies beyond the immediate gains and losses of the financial world—a place where shadows give way to light.

Amidst the maze of numbers and transactions, there is a subtle shift in perception, a moment when the relentless pursuit of profit pauses, allowing for a glimpse into something more profound. It's as if the city itself breathes a sigh of relief, revealing a landscape untouched by the frenetic pace of modern economics. Here, the golden hues of a setting sun cast long shadows across the polished marble floors of a grand old bank, illuminating the intricate carvings of its columns and the stories they silently tell.

Within this hallowed space, the air is thick with the scent of aged leather and polished wood, mingling with the faint trace of ink and paper—a sensory reminder of the legacy that preceded the digital age. The whispers of past transactions linger, a testament to the generations who walked these halls, each leaving their indelible mark on the fabric of financial history.

In the quiet corners of this sanctuary, where the noise of the outside world fades into a distant murmur, there is a sense of clarity. Here, the figures on a balance sheet transform into narratives of ambition, risk, and resilience. The columns and rows become more than mere data; they become the lifeblood of dreams realized and dreams deferred.

A solitary figure stands in the center of this space, silhouetted against the warm glow of the setting sun. Their eyes scan the room, absorbing the intricate tapestry of past and present. In their hand, a worn ledger book, its pages filled with the meticulous records of transactions long past, each entry a testament to the choices that shaped fortunes and futures.

As the light continues to shift, it reveals the hidden beauty in the mundane— the play of shadows on a brass doorknob, the delicate dance of dust motes in a sunbeam. In these moments, there is a profound realization that beyond the immediate pressures and demands of the financial world, there lies a deeper understanding of value, one that transcends monetary gain.

It is a place where the human element reclaims its rightful place amidst the algorithms and analytics, where the stories of individuals and communities come to the forefront. It is here that the intangible assets of trust, integrity, and vision are recognized as the true currency of enduring success.

In this quiet revelation, the light beyond the shadows becomes not just a metaphor, but a tangible reality—a guiding beacon for those willing to look beyond the surface and into the heart of what truly matters. As the sun dips below the horizon, leaving behind a soft afterglow, there is a sense that this journey into the light has only just begun, promising new horizons yet to be explored.

# Chapter 8: The Cost of Ambition

## *The Drive Within*

In the dimly lit corridors of the bustling city, where shadows of towering skyscrapers stretch across the streets like outstretched fingers, the pulse of ambition beats relentlessly. The air is thick with the scent of opportunity mingled with the faint aroma of desperation, a cocktail that fuels the fire within those who dare to chase dreams amidst the financial labyrinth. Beneath the shimmering facade of glass and steel lies a world where fortunes are made and lost, a world that demands more than just skill—it demands an intrinsic drive that propels individuals forward, even when the odds seem insurmountable.

The city, a living organism in its own right, hums with the energy of countless souls striving to carve their mark. Among them is Alex, a figure silhouetted against the backdrop of neon lights, his silhouette a testament to the relentless pursuit of success. His eyes, sharp and focused, betray a hunger that many recognize but few truly comprehend. It is the hunger of one who has tasted the bitterness of failure and yet rises each morning with renewed resolve, fueled by the whispers of potential that echo in the recesses of his mind.

The financial district, with its labyrinthine network of streets and alleys, is both a playground and a battlefield. Here, the line between triumph and defeat is as thin as a stock ticker, and the stakes are as high as the soaring skyscrapers that pierce the sky. Alex navigates this world with the deftness of a seasoned sailor, his instincts honed by years of experience in the unforgiving seas of commerce. His office, perched high above the bustling streets, is a sanctuary where strategies are conceived, risks are calculated, and dreams are molded into reality.

In the quiet solitude of his office, Alex sits at his desk, the glow of his computer screen illuminating the determined lines etched into his face. His fingers dance across the keyboard, orchestrating a symphony of numbers and projections, a delicate balance between logic and intuition. Each keystroke is a step closer to his vision, a testament to the drive that courses through his veins like a relentless current.

Outside, the city continues its ceaseless rhythm, a cacophony of sounds that blend into a symphony of ambition. The streets teem with people, each one a story unfolding amidst the concrete and steel. For

Alex, these streets are more than just pathways; they are veins through which the lifeblood of commerce flows. They are the stage upon which he performs the intricate dance of finance, a dance that requires both grace and grit.

As the sun sets, casting long shadows across the city, Alex stands at the window, gazing out at the sprawling metropolis before him. The twinkling lights below are a testament to the countless dreams that flicker in the hearts of those who, like him, are driven by an unyielding desire to succeed. In this world where shadows and light play an eternal game of cat and mouse, it is the drive within that separates the dreamers from the doers. And for Alex, the journey is far from over.

## *Sacrifices Made*

The room was dimly lit, shrouded in a haze of nostalgia and untold stories. The soft glow of a single lamp cast elongated shadows on the walls, echoing the theme of the book that lay open on the desk. An air of solemnity enveloped the space, as if the very walls were whispering tales of the sacrifices made in pursuit of financial stability.

A worn leather chair stood in the corner, its creases and wrinkles narrating the passage of time, much like the man who often occupied it. He was a figure molded by years of dedication and relentless pursuit, his face a canvas of lines etched by perseverance. Each wrinkle bore witness to sleepless nights, each crease a testament to the dreams deferred and the moments missed.

On the desk, a collection of photographs lay scattered, each capturing a fragment of a life once vibrant and full of promise. In one, a young family smiled brightly, their eyes gleaming with hope and ambition. In another, a man stood alone, his expression a mixture of pride and resignation, the weight of his choices visible in his stooped shoulders.

The clock ticked softly in the background, its rhythmic sound a constant reminder of time slipping away, much like the opportunities that had once seemed endless. Yet, in this quiet sanctuary, there was a profound sense of acceptance, as if the sacrifices made were not in vain but rather stepping stones toward a future yet to unfold.

Books lined the shelves, their spines a kaleidoscope of colors and titles. Each one was a gateway to knowledge and understanding, yet each also a reminder of the hours spent in solitude, engrossed in study and self-

51

improvement. The man had traded laughter-filled evenings for quiet nights with these books, hoping they would guide him toward the financial security he so desperately sought.

Outside the window, the world seemed to move at a frenetic pace, oblivious to the quiet battles fought within these four walls. The city lights flickered like a distant constellation, each one representing a dream, a sacrifice, a story untold. The bustling streets were filled with people chasing similar dreams, each unaware of the sacrifices made by those around them.

In the end, the sacrifices were not merely about financial gain but about the transformation of the self. Each decision, each moment of struggle, had shaped a man who understood the true value of what he had pursued. The sacrifices made were not measured in dollars and cents but in the growth of character and the resilience forged in the crucible of experience.

As the evening deepened into night, the man sat in quiet reflection, a sense of peace settling over him. He knew that  the path he had chosen was fraught with challenges, but it was a path that had taught him the importance of perseverance,  the beauty of quiet strength, and the profound impact of the sacrifices he had made. And in that realization, he found solace, knowing that the shadows cast by his sacrifices were not dark and foreboding but rather a testament to the light they had brought into his life.

## *The Invisible Toll*

Beneath the surface of financial transactions and economic calculations lies a realm often overlooked—a domain where the intangible costs of monetary decisions silently accrue. This hidden layer of expenses, though unseen, exerts a profound influence on both individuals and societies.

Within the bustling streets of any metropolis, where towering skyscrapers house the epicenters of commerce, there exists a palpable tension. The atmosphere is charged with the anticipation of gains and losses, yet the cost that silently shadows every transaction remains largely unacknowledged. This is the invisible toll, a fee extracted not in currency but in the subtler currencies of stress, time, and opportunity.

Consider the young professional, ensconced in the cocoon of a corporate cubicle, eyes glued to the flickering glow of a computer screen. The ticker tape of the stock market scrolls endlessly, numbers rising and falling like the tides. Each decision, each click of the mouse, carries with it an unseen weight. Beyond the immediate financial implications, there is a mental burden, a psychological levy that compounds over time.

Beyond the individual, the invisible toll extends its reach into the very fabric of communities. In neighborhoods where economic disparity is as stark as the contrasting hues of dawn and dusk, the weight is palpable. The relentless pursuit of financial stability can fracture communal bonds, breeding an environment where cooperation gives way to competition. Here, the cost is measured in frayed relationships and lost trust, a currency as valuable as it is intangible.

In the realm of global finance, the invisible toll manifests as the unseen consequences of policy decisions. A change in

interest rates or trade agreements ripple through economies, affecting livelihoods in ways that are not immediately apparent. The long-term impact on employment, education, and social welfare often remains hidden beneath the surface, only to emerge as a specter of regret in the annals of history.

The digital age, with its promise of instantaneous transactions and global connectivity, further complicates this landscape. In the quest for convenience, the subtleties of human interaction are often sacrificed at the altar of efficiency. The click of a button, the swipe of a screen—each action severs a thread in the intricate web of personal connections, exacting a toll on the currency of human experience.

Yet, amidst this unseen calculus, there exists an opportunity for awareness. By recognizing the invisible toll, individuals and societies can begin to mitigate its effects. This requires a shift in perspective, an acknowledgment that not all costs are monetary and that the true value of a decision often lies in its broader impact.

In this complex tapestry of financial existence, the invisible toll serves as a reminder of the delicate balance between progress and preservation. It calls for a mindful approach, where the pursuit of wealth is tempered by the wisdom of foresight and the understanding that some costs, though invisible, are all too real. In navigating the shadows of finance, it is this awareness that lights the path forward, illuminating the hidden costs that accompany the pursuit of prosperity.

# The Price of Dreams

The city was a living organism, pulsating with the ceaseless hum of ambition and the relentless pursuit of success. In the midst of towering skyscrapers and bustling streets, dreams were traded like commodities, each with its own value, its own allure. The neon lights reflected off the glass facades, casting a kaleidoscope of colors that danced across the faces of those who dared to chase their aspirations.

In this urban jungle, every corner held a story, every alley whispered secrets of triumphs and failures. The air was thick with the scent of opportunity, mingling with the aroma of street food and the exhaust of countless vehicles. It was a place where dreams could be born anew or shattered with a single decision.

Amidst the cacophony, there was a rhythm, a beat that dictated the pace of life. It was a symphony composed of the clatter of footsteps, the honking of horns, and the distant wail of sirens. It was the soundtrack of a city that never slept, a city that thrived on the dreams of its inhabitants.

For those who dared to dream, the cost was not always measured in currency. It was paid in sleepless nights and endless days, in the sacrifice of time with loved ones and the relinquishing of comfort. It demanded resilience, a fierce determination that burned brighter than the city lights.

The dreamers were a diverse tapestry, woven together by their shared pursuit of something greater. There were the young and the old, the hopeful and the weary, each driven by their own vision of success. They navigated the labyrinth of opportunity, where every turn could lead to fortune or despair.

In the shadows of the financial district, deals were struck and fortunes were made. The air buzzed with the tension of negotiations, each word carefully chosen, each gesture calculated. It was a world where the stakes were high, and the price of failure was steep.

Yet, amidst the chaos, there was beauty. In the glint of sunlight off glass and steel, in the laughter shared over coffee in a crowded café, in the quiet moments of reflection as the city skyline shimmered in the distance. These were the moments that made the price of dreams bearable, the moments that reminded the dreamers of the reason they embarked on this journey.

The city was a tapestry of contrasts, a place where dreams were both nurtured and challenged. It was a reminder that the path to success was rarely a straight line, but rather a winding road filled with unexpected detours and hidden treasures.

In the end, the price of dreams was a reflection of the value placed upon them. For some, it was a burden too heavy to bear, while for others, it was a testament to their unwavering belief in a future yet to be realized. The city stood as a testament to the resilience of the human spirit, a beacon for those who dared to dream, and a reminder that even in the shadows, there was light.

# Chapter 9: The Veil of Security

## *The Illusory Shield*

In the heart of the bustling metropolis, where skyscrapers clawed at the overcast sky, a peculiar sense of security wrapped its tendrils around the inhabitants. The streets below, alive with the hum of commerce and the rhythm of hurried footsteps, painted a vivid picture of prosperity. Yet, beneath the surface of this thriving urban tapestry, a delicate web of financial intricacies lay hidden, cloaked in an illusory shield of stability.

The city, with its towering financial institutions and glittering storefronts, exuded an aura of invincibility. To the untrained eye, wealth seemed as abundant as the rain that occasionally swept in from the distant coast, refreshing the air with its presence. But within the gleaming facades of banks and investment firms, an invisible dance of numbers played out, weaving a narrative far more complex than the outward appearance suggested.

Amidst this landscape, individuals moved like pieces on a grand chessboard, each believing they held a winning strategy. From the ambitious entrepreneur launching a startup in a trendy loft, to the seasoned investor poring over stock charts in a corner office, there was a shared confidence that the financial fortress they inhabited was impenetrable.

Yet, the shield that protected them was not forged from impenetrable steel, but rather from fragile illusions. It was a concept built on assumptions and projections, on faith in the systems that governed their monetary world. The media, with its glossy reports and optimistic forecasts, perpetuated the myth of unending growth, lulling the populace into a sense of comfort.

Behind closed doors, financial wizards and analysts whispered of potential storms, their voices drowned out by the clamor of the market's relentless march forward. This was a world where risk was calculated, yet often dismissed, where the language of derivatives and leverage became an embroidery of complexity that few dared untangle.

In the corridors of power, decisions were made that could tilt the balance of this intricate dance. Policies enacted with the stroke of a pen could ripple through the economy, affecting lives in ways unseen and unanticipated. Yet, the aura of security persisted, a comforting mirage that shielded the masses from the harsh realities that lurked beneath.

As daylight faded and the cityscape was bathed in the golden hues of twilight, the financial shadows lengthened, casting a veil over the bustling streets. It was in these shadows that the true nature of the illusory shield revealed itself—a delicate balance, ever teetering on the edge of collapse, held together by trust as fragile as the wisps of smoke rising from the chimneys of the distant industrial district.

In this world of financial shadows, the line between security and vulnerability was thin, a tightrope walk performed daily by those who dared to navigate its complexities. And while the city continued to shine with its facade of prosperity, the undercurrent of uncertainty remained, a constant reminder that the shield, though comforting, was but an illusion waiting to be shattered by the unseen forces of change.

## Cracks in the Armor

In the dim glow of the early morning, the city streets bore a peculiar silence, punctuated only by the occasional clatter of a distant train or the faint hum of traffic. This silence was deceptive, cloaking the bustling undercurrents of its financial district. Here, in the shadowy corners of towering skyscrapers, the true essence of the city was captured—not in the grandeur of its architecture but in the fragility of its foundations.

Amidst the colossal edifices of glass and steel, figures moved with a purpose, their silhouettes cast against the rising sun. These were the brokers, the analysts, the investors—each carrying the weight of their ambitions and the burden of their fears. Their paths intersected in the labyrinth of corridors and elevators, where whispered conversations held the power to shape fortunes and futures.

Within the confines of a polished boardroom, the atmosphere was thick with anticipation. The room was a blend of opulence and austerity, with its mahogany table and leather chairs standing as silent witnesses to countless negotiations. Yet, beneath the veneer of success, tension simmered, as if the very walls could sense the precariousness of the empire it housed.

At the center of this unfolding drama was a man whose presence commanded attention. His eyes, sharp and calculating, scanned the room with an intensity that belied his calm demeanor. He was a figure of authority, a titan in the world of finance, yet there was an imperceptible crack in his facade—a momentary flicker of doubt that betrayed the certainty he projected.

The meeting commenced, a symphony of voices rising and falling in a delicate dance of persuasion and resistance. Each participant was acutely aware of the stakes, their words carefully chosen, their expressions meticulously controlled. Yet, as the discussions progressed, subtle shifts in tone and posture hinted at underlying unease.

Outside, the city remained oblivious to the machinations within. The sun climbed higher, casting long shadows across the facades of buildings, as if echoing the hidden vulnerabilities within their walls. Pedestrians hurried past, their footsteps echoing on the pavement, unaware of the delicate balance being negotiated above.

Back in the boardroom, the discourse reached a crescendo. The once seamless harmony now showed signs of discord, as voices rose in urgency and the air grew charged with tension. It was here, in these moments of heightened emotion, that the cracks in the armor became most apparent.

The man at the helm, once unyielding, now seemed to bear the weight of his decisions more heavily. His gaze, once unwavering, now flickered with uncertainty, as if the shadows of doubt had crept into his consciousness. It was a silent acknowledgment of the precariousness of their situation, a recognition that even the most fortified defenses could be breached.

As the meeting drew to a close, the participants filed out, their faces a mask of composure, yet their minds undoubtedly racing with thoughts of what lay ahead. The room, now empty, retained the echoes of their conversations, a testament to the fragility of the constructs they had built.

Outside, the city continued its relentless pace, oblivious to the cracks that had begun to form beneath its surface. In the quiet moments that followed, the true nature of the financial world was laid bare—not as an impregnable fortress but as a delicate structure constantly teetering on the brink of collapse.

## The Hidden Vulnerabilities

In the vast expanse of the financial realm, beneath the gleaming surface of prosperity and growth, lie intricacies hidden from the untrained eye. These nuances, often overlooked, harbor vulnerabilities capable of shaking the very foundations of economic stability.

Within the labyrinth of numbers and charts, a delicate balance is maintained. This balance, much like a tightrope walker swaying with each gust of wind, can be easily disrupted by unseen forces. As the world becomes increasingly interconnected, the very systems designed to safeguard financial integrity become potential conduits for unforeseen risks.

Consider the intricate web of global supply chains, which, while fostering efficiency, also create dependencies. A single disruption in this chain, whether due to geopolitical tensions or natural disasters, can ripple across continents, affecting economies large and small. The fragility of these networks is a testament to the hidden vulnerabilities that lurk beneath the surface.

Moreover, the digital transformation of financial systems, while ushering in an era of unprecedented convenience and speed, introduces a new set of challenges. Cybersecurity threats loom large, with hackers probing for weaknesses in the armor of financial institutions. A breach, beyond the immediate financial loss, can erode trust—a currency that is invaluable in the financial world.

In the realm of investments, the pursuit of profit often blinds stakeholders to the latent risks. The allure of high returns can overshadow the peril of volatile markets, where swift changes in sentiment can lead to precipitous declines. The speculative nature of certain assets, especially in emerging markets, adds another layer of complexity, with investors sometimes finding themselves in perilous waters without a lifeline.

Equally significant is the shadow banking system, operating outside traditional regulatory frameworks. These entities are less transparent by nature, making them susceptible to liquidity crises. The opacity of these operations can mask systemic risks, which, if left unchecked, may culminate in financial upheaval.

The human element, too, plays a pivotal role in the unfolding of financial vulnerabilities. Behavioral biases, such asoverconfidence or herd mentality, can exacerbate market fluctuations. Decision-makers, swayed by emotions rather than rational analysis, may inadvertently steer financial ships into turbulent waters.

Regulatory frameworks, designed to mitigate these vulnerabilities, often find themselves lagging behind the rapid pace of financial innovation. The challenge lies in crafting policies that are both robust and adaptable, capable of addressing the multifaceted nature of modern financial systems.

As these hidden vulnerabilities persist, they serve as a reminder of the inherent uncertainties within financial ecosystems. Vigilance becomes imperative, as does the continual adaptation of strategies to mitigate risks. The financial shadows, though elusive, cast long and profound effects, shaping the trajectory of economic landscapes.

In navigating these complexities, a nuanced understanding of the hidden vulnerabilities is essential. It is only through acknowledging and addressing these unseen forces that the financial world can hope to achieve enduring stability and resilience.

## Unveiling the Truth

The room was dimly lit, casting long shadows that seemed to stretch and yawn across the polished wooden floor. A faint hum of fluorescent lights buzzed overhead, mingling with the soft rustle of papers being shuffled by anxious hands. In the center of this hushed chaos sat an imposing mahogany table, its surface gleaming with the sheen of meticulous care. Around it, faces etched with a mixture of anticipation and trepidation gathered, eyes darting to the centerpiece of attention – a thick, leather-bound dossier.

This was no ordinary meeting; it was a clandestine congregation drawn by the allure of a truth long buried beneath layers of financial sleight of hand. The dossier, a repository of secrets, lay there like a dormant volcano, ready to erupt with revelations that could shake the very foundations of their world. It was a compilation of whispers and rumors, of ledgers and logs that spoke of transactions shrouded in mystery and intrigue.

As the custodian of this Pandora's box of financial shadows, Victoria sat at the head of the table, her demeanor calm yet authoritative. Her fingers traced the edges of the dossier, each touch a promise of what lay within. Her eyes, sharp and discerning, scanned the room, meeting each gaze with a silent assurance that the truth would be unveiled, no matter the cost.

The air was thick with anticipation, charged with the electricity of imminent discovery. Each person present was acutely aware of the implications, of the potential fallout that could ensue once the contents of the dossier were laid bare. Yet, there was no turning back. The time had come to peel back the layers of deception, to confront the shadows that had long lingered in the corridors of power.

With a deliberate, steady hand, Victoria opened the dossier, revealing pages upon pages of meticulously documented evidence. The room seemed to hold its breath as she began to speak, her voice steady and clear, a beacon cutting through the fog of uncertainty. She spoke of shell companies and offshore accounts, of money trails that twisted and turned like a serpent weaving through a labyrinth.

Her words painted a vivid picture, each detail a brushstroke on the canvas of corruption. She described the intricate web of deceit spun by those who had manipulated the system to their advantage, who had cloaked their actions in the guise of legitimacy while siphoning off fortunes into the shadows. The room listened in rapt silence, each revelation landing like a hammer blow, each truth a chisel chipping away at the facade of respectability.

As Victoria laid bare the intricacies of this financial underworld, the gravity of the situation became increasingly apparent. Faces around the table shifted from shock to understanding, from disbelief to resolve. It was clear that the path forward would not be easy, but it was a path that had to be taken. The truth, once hidden, now stood exposed in all its stark reality, a testament to the power of perseverance and the relentless pursuit of justice.

As the meeting drew to a close, the shadows in the room seemed to recede, replaced by a newfound clarity and purpose. The dossier, once a symbol of hidden truths, now served as a catalyst for change, a reminder that even in the darkest corners of finance, the light of truth could still prevail.

# Chapter 10: Shadows of the Future

## *Glimpses Ahead*

The horizon of financial landscapes is ever-shifting, a dynamic tableau painted with the hues of uncertainty and opportunity. As we stand at this precipice of change, the shadows cast by economic forces stretch long and wide, blending with the light of innovation and ambition.

In this intricate dance of shadows, the global economy unfurls its patterns, weaving through the fabric of time with the threads of policy, technology, and human endeavor. This is a realm where the past informs the present, and the present shapes the future, each moment a brushstroke in a vast and complex mural.

As we gaze into the future, the outlines of emerging trends begin to take shape, their forms both familiar and novel. The digital revolution continues to redefine the boundaries of commerce and finance, as blockchain technology and cryptocurrencies carve new paths through traditional systems. These digital assets, once mere whispers on the fringes of economic discourse, now stand poised to transform the very essence of financial transactions, challenging the status quo, and inviting speculation.

Yet, within these shadows lies the specter of volatility. The very innovations that promise growth and prosperity also harbor risks that must be navigated with care. Regulatory frameworks struggle to keep pace with rapid advancements, creating a landscape where uncertainty looms large. The interplay between regulation and innovation becomes a delicate balance, a tightrope walk upon which the future of finance precariously teeters.

Globalization, too, casts its shadow, both a catalyst for growth and a harbinger of complexity. As markets intertwine, the ripple effects of decisions made in one corner of the world can be felt across continents. The interconnectedness of economies demands a nuanced understanding, where local actions resonate on a global scale. The challenge lies in harnessing this interconnectedness for collective benefit while mitigating the risks inherent in such a tightly woven tapestry.

Amidst these overarching themes, the human element remains constant. Individuals' aspirations, fears, and ambitions drive the engines of economies, their stories interwoven with the broader narratives of markets and nations. As we peer into the future, it is the human capacity for resilience, innovation, and adaptation that offers the most profound glimpses of what lies ahead.

In this unfolding narrative, the role of leaders and policymakers becomes paramount. Their decisions, informed by both data and intuition, will chart the course through these shadows. The challenge is to create frameworks that foster innovation while safeguarding stability, to embrace change without losing sight of the fundamental principles that underpin economic well-being.

In the midst of uncertainty, there is a promise—a promise of growth, of progress, and of a future shaped by the collective will to navigate these financial shadows. As we stand on the cusp of this new era, the path forward is illuminated not just by the light of innovation but also by the shadows that compel us to look deeper, to understand more profoundly, and to act with wisdom and foresight. Here, in the interplay of light and shadow, the future awaits, offering glimpses of a world yet to be fully realized.

## *The Uncertain Path*

A dense fog cloaked the cityscape, blurring the boundaries between reality and illusion. The shadows of skyscrapers stretched across the ground like long fingers reaching into the abyss, creating a landscape that felt both familiar and foreign. In this world of financial shadows, every decision seemed to carry the weight of the unknown, where the line between success and failure was as thin as a razor's edge.

The air was thick with the scent of possibility mixed with the pungent aroma of risk. Here, in the heart of the financial district, the hum of activity was relentless. Traders, investors, and analysts moved with a frenetic energy, their faces etched with determination and anxiety. Each step they took was laden with the hopes of prosperity, yet tinged with the fear of ruin.

The streets were a maze of ambition, where each turn could lead to fortune or folly. Conversations buzzed with jargon that seemed almost like a foreign language to the uninitiated. Words like "derivatives," "hedging," and "leverage" floated through the air, each carrying a promise of great rewards or devastating losses.

In the midst of this chaotic symphony, there was a sense of isolation. Despite the throngs of people, each individual was locked in their own world, navigating the labyrinthine corridors of finance with a singular focus. The pursuit of wealth was an all-consuming endeavor, demanding sacrifices that often went unnoticed by those outside this sphere.

Windows of towering office buildings glimmered in the muted light, reflecting the aspirations of those within. Behind these glass facades, decisions were made that could alter the fate of markets and livelihoods. The unseen forces at play were like currents beneath the surface of a turbulent sea, invisible yet profoundly influential.

Yet, amidst the uncertainty, there was a strange allure. The financial world was a stage where fortunes were made and lost in the blink of an eye. It was a place where the audacious could rise to unimaginable heights, propelled by a daring move or a calculated risk. But for every success story, there were countless tales of those who had wandered too close to the edge, only to be swallowed by the shadows.

The city, with its towering edifices and ceaseless activity, was a testament to the resilience and resourcefulness of those who dared to traverse this uncertain path. It was a place where dreams were both realized and shattered, where the price of ambition was measured in sleepless nights and anxious days.

In the end, the allure of the financial shadows lay in their unpredictability. The path was never straight, but this uncertainty fueled the determination of those who walked it. Each step was a dance with destiny, a delicate balance between caution and courage. The shadows may have loomed large, but for those with the fortitude to face them, they held the promise of a brighter future just beyond the horizon.

## Navigating the Unknown

In the dimly lit corridors of financial uncertainty lies a landscape that is both daunting and exhilarating. The world of finance, with its intricate web of numbers and possibilities, often presents itself as a labyrinth where every twist and turn carries hidden risks and potential rewards. This chapter delves into the heart of these uncharted territories, where the shadows of doubt loom large, yet the allure of discovery never fades.

The unknown in finance is a vast ocean, its surface occasionally disrupted by the ripples of market fluctuations and economic shifts. Beneath these waves lie the depths of ambiguity, where traditional metrics and forecasts struggle to reach. Here, intuition and insight become invaluable compasses, guiding those daring enough to venture into this enigmatic realm. It is in this space that pioneers of finance find themselves, equipped with a blend of analytical prowess and an unyielding curiosity.

As one steps into this realm, the landscape is marked by the ever-present specter of volatility. Markets ebb and flow like tides, each movement carrying with it the potential to reshape fortunes. The challenge is not merely to withstand these waves but to harness them, turning uncertainty into opportunity. This requires a keen understanding of the forces at play, an ability to discern patterns amidst chaos, and the foresight to anticipate shifts before they occur.

In the shadows of uncertainty, risk management emerges as both an art and a science. It is here that the delicate balance of caution and boldness is struck. The adept navigator of financial unknowns understands that risk cannot be eliminated but rather mitigated, transformed into a calculated gamble that can yield substantial returns. This involves a meticulous assessment of potential outcomes, a strategic allocation of resources, and an unwavering readiness to adapt as new information surfaces.

The unknown also presents a canvas for innovation. As traditional paradigms falter under the weight of unforeseen challenges, the opportunity for creative solutions arises. Financial innovators, driven by a desire to forge new paths, harness technology and unconventional strategies to chart courses previously deemed impossible. In doing so, they not only redefine the boundaries of what is achievable but also inspire others to follow suit, each step forward illuminating the path for those behind.

Yet, amidst the allure of exploration, the human element remains a constant. Emotions, biases, and perceptions weave their way into decision-making processes, sometimes clouding judgment, other times providing clarity. The successful navigator acknowledges these influences, striving to maintain a balance between objective analysis and emotional intelligence. It is this harmony that allows for decisions that are both informed and intuitive, grounded in reality yet open to the possibilities that lie beyond.

In the end, navigating the unknown in finance is a journey of perpetual learning and adaptation. It is a domain where the only certainty is change, and the path forward is illuminated by the flickering light of experience and insight. For those who dare to tread this path, the rewards are not solely financial; they encompass the satisfaction of mastering complexity, the thrill of discovery, and the enduring quest for understanding in a world defined by shadows.

# The Dawn of Possibilities

The city awoke with a soft murmur as the first light of dawn began to cast its golden hue over the horizon, illuminating the once shadowed corners of the bustling metropolis. The financial district, a labyrinth of towering skyscrapers and winding streets, started to pulse with life, its energy palpable even from a distance. As the sun climbed higher, its rays danced off glass façades and steel structures, painting a kaleidoscope of reflections on the pavement below.

Amidst this awakening, a sense of anticipation hung in the air. Traders and brokers, clad in tailored suits, hurried along the sidewalks with purpose, their footsteps echoing the rhythm of the city's heartbeat. The stock exchange, a formidable edifice

of power and influence, stood at the center of it all, its marble pillars gleaming in the morning light. Inside, the trading floor was a hive of activity, its atmosphere charged with the electric potential of the day ahead.

From the novice investor to the seasoned financier, everyone felt the shift. It was as if the universe had tilted slightly, opening a window to opportunities previously veiled by uncertainty and doubt. The financial world, often shrouded in complexity and risk, now appeared as a vast landscape of untapped potential.

In the midst of this awakening, a young analyst named Emma stood at the edge of her own possibilities. Her cubicle, nestled among the rows of desks, was a testament to her journey thus far—a collection of charts, reports, and post-it notes that told a story of late nights and hard-won insights. Today, however, she sensed a change. The air was thick with the promise of something new, a whisper of innovation that beckoned her towards uncharted territories.

Emma's gaze drifted to the sprawling cityscape outside her window, where the morning light played upon the buildings like a symphony of colors. In that moment, she realized that beneath the surface of financial shadows lay a world brimming with potential. The data she analyzed daily was not just numbers on a screen, but the heartbeat of economies, the pulse of progress.

With a renewed sense of purpose, Emma turned back to her work, her mind alight with ideas. She saw patterns where others saw chaos, opportunities where others saw obstacles. The dawn of possibilities was not just a metaphor, but a reality waiting to be explored. As the morning unfolded into afternoon, she found herself at the forefront of a new wave, riding the crest of innovation towards a future she had only dared to imagine.

Outside, the city continued its dance, a harmonious blend of ambition and aspiration. The financial shadows, once a daunting maze, now seemed like a canvas upon which new narratives could be painted. Emma knew that the journey ahead would be fraught with challenges, but the promise of discovery outweighed the fear of the unknown.

As the sun set and the city bathed in twilight, the dawn of possibilities lingered in the air, an ever-present reminder of the transformative power of vision and determination. In that quiet moment, Emma understood that the true essence of progress lay not in the shadows of uncertainty but in the courage to step into the light of possibility.

# Chapter 11: The Weight of Choices

## *The Fork in the Road*

Silence wrapped around the dimly lit room like a heavy cloak, the only sound the rhythmic ticking of a vintage clock perched on the mantelpiece. The room was an eclectic mix of eras, with a sleek, modern desk juxtaposed against the backdrop of faded floral wallpaper that had seen better days. The air was thick with the scent of old paper and a hint of sandalwood, evoking memories of forgotten libraries and dusty tomes.

In the center of the room stood a figure, cloaked in the shadows cast by the waning afternoon sun that filtered through the half-drawn curtains. His eyes, dark and contemplative, were fixed on the piece of paper lying on the desk before him. It was a letter, its edges slightly crumpled from being read and reread countless times. The words, scrawled in a hurried hand, seemed to leap off the page, each sentence a whisper of possibilities yet unexplored.

Outside, the city was a cacophony of life, bustling with the energy of a thousand stories unfolding simultaneously. Yet here, in this small sanctuary, time seemed to stand still, holding its breath as if waiting for a decision to be made. The letter was an invitation, a call to step into the unknown, to leave behind the familiar confines of routine and comfort. It spoke of opportunities, risks, and the tantalizing allure of a future unshackled by the weight of past failures.

The man's mind was a whirlpool of thoughts, each one colliding with the next in a chaotic dance. Visions of what could be flitted through his consciousness—a life reimagined, unburdened by the shadows of financial missteps and lingering disappointments. Yet, with each tantalizing possibility came the specter of uncertainty, the fear of stepping onto a path without a clear destination in sight.

He moved to the window, pushing aside the heavy drapes to peer out at the world below. The street was alive with movement, people hurrying past with determined strides, each one lost in their own narrative. The sight was both comforting and isolating, a reminder that he was but one of many standing at a crossroads, each choice a thread in the intricate tapestry of life.

A deep sigh escaped his lips, the sound barely audible over the hum of the city beyond. He turned back to the letter, the weight of its promise pressing down on him. The choice was his alone to make, a solitary decision that would ripple through the fabric of his existence, altering its course in ways yet unseen.

The clock ticked on, each second a gentle reminder that time, relentless and unyielding, waits for no one. Yet, in this moment of quiet reflection, there was a clarity that had eluded him before. It was not the fear of failure that held him back, but the fear of change, of stepping into a realm where the shadows of the past could not follow.

With a steady hand, he reached for a pen, the weight of it familiar and comforting. The ink flowed smoothly as he began to write, each word a step toward a future that beckoned with both promise and uncertainty. The road ahead was unknown, yet for the first time in a long while, he felt a flicker of hope— a light in the financial shadows that had long shrouded his dreams.

## The Pull of Options

A faint rustle echoed through the cavernous halls of the stock exchange, a symphony of whispers that danced between the marble columns and the polished wooden floors. Traders, like choreographed marionettes, moved with a rhythm only they understood, eyes glued to the flickering screens that painted their faces with hues of green and red. Amidst this orchestrated chaos, the allure of options trading shimmered like a mirage, promising both fortune and folly in equal measure.The novice trader, Alex, stood on the periphery, a silent observer in a world that felt both foreign and familiar. To Alex, the concept of options was an enigma, a cryptic language that spoke of possibilities rather than certainties. It was the financial equivalent of alchemy, transforming the mundane into the magical with a mere stroke of a pen.

Options, with their seductive complexity, were like the sirens of ancient myths, calling traders to the rocky shores of risk with promises of untold wealth. They offered a tantalizing escape from the monotony of traditional investing, where the rules were rigid and the returns predictable. In contrast, options were fluid and malleable, bending to the will of those who dared to wield them.

As Alex delved deeper into the world of options, the allure only intensified. The language of calls and puts, strikes and expirations, became a symphony of potential outcomes, each note resonating with the promise of profit or the specter of loss. It was a game of chess played on a vast and ever-shifting board, where strategy and intuition danced in delicate harmony.

The seasoned traders navigated this landscape with the precision of master craftsmen, their eyes scanning the horizon for the slightest hint of opportunity. They spoke in hushed tones, exchanging insights and strategies like seasoned generals planning a campaign. The air was thick with tension, an electric charge that crackled with the anticipation of what lay ahead.

Each option contract was a story waiting to be told, a narrative written in numbers and probabilities. For Alex, the challenge was to decipher these tales, to unravel the threads of uncertainty that wove through the fabric of each trade. It was a task that required both intellect and instinct, a delicate balance between logic and intuition.

The world of options was not for the faint of heart. It demanded a willingness to embrace the unknown, to dance on the edge of risk with the confidence of a tightrope walker. Yet, for those who mastered its intricacies, the rewards were as boundless as the horizon itself.

In this realm of financial shadows, options stood as both a beacon and a warning. They offered a glimpse into a world where possibilities were endless, where the only limits were those imposed by one's imagination. Yet, they also served as a reminder of the perils that lurked beneath the surface, waiting to ensnare the unwary in their intricate web.

For Alex, the pull of options was irresistible, a siren's call that beckoned with the promise of adventure and discovery. It was a journey into the unknown, a voyage through the uncharted waters of finance where the only certainty was the thrill of the chase. And so, with a mixture of trepidation and excitement,

Alex stepped into the world of options, ready to embrace the challenge and explore the limitless potential that lay ahead.

## Decisions and Consequences

In the dim light of the office, the air hung heavy with the weight of unspoken possibilities. A low hum from the city below seeped through the open window, a constant reminder of the world that continued to turn, indifferent to the turmoil within. As the clock ticked its steady beat, decisions loomed like dark clouds on the horizon, casting long shadows that threatened to engulf everything in their path.

Each choice, no matter how small, seemed to carry with it the potential to alter the course of lives, as if the universe itself were holding its breath, waiting to see which path would be taken. The ledger lay open on the desk, its columns of numbers like soldiers standing in solemn rows, each figure a testament to past decisions and the consequences they had wrought.

For James, the protagonist of our tale, the moment was fraught with tension. His fingers drummed a restless tattoo on the mahogany surface, eyes scanning the figures with a mixture of hope and dread. The financial shadows that stretched before him were not merely projections on a spreadsheet; they were specters of his past choices, each one a reminder of opportunities seized or squandered.

In the world of finance, decisions were rarely black and white. They were shades of gray, nuanced and complex, each one a gamble with stakes that could not be easily calculated. The allure of potential gain was ever-present, seductive, and shimmering just out of reach. Yet, the specter of loss loomed large, its presence a constant reminder of the fragility of ambition.

As James pondered his options, the weight of responsibility pressed down upon him. He knew that his decisions would ripple outward, affecting not only his own future but the lives of countless others who depended on his judgment. In this world of financial shadows, every choice was a step into the unknown, a leap of faith into a void where certainty was elusive and risk was the only constant.

The consequences of past decisions lingered, like ghosts haunting the corridors of his mind. He recalled the moment when he had taken that first bold step into the world of high finance, wide-eyed and full of dreams. It had been a world of promise then, a landscape ripe with potential. But as time wore on, the sheen of possibility had dulled, replaced by the harsh realities of a world that demanded sacrifices. Yet, amidst the uncertainty, there was a glimmer of hope. James understood that while decisions carried the potential for loss, they also held the promise of redemption. Each choice was an opportunity to learn, to grow, to forge a new path through the shifting shadows.

As he sat there, poised on the precipice of a decision that could change everything, James allowed himself a moment of reflection. He understood that the path forward was not always clear, that the shadows could be deceiving, hiding both danger and opportunity in their depths. But he also knew that it was within his power to shape his own destiny, to navigate the labyrinthine world of finance with courage and conviction.

And so, with a steadying breath, he reached for the pen, ready to inscribe his choice onto the pages of his life, knowing that whatever the outcome, he would face it with resolve, ready to embrace the consequences of his decisions.

## Paths Taken and Lost

In the dim glow of a fading autumn sun, the streets of the financial district lay like a labyrinth of choices, each path intertwining with the next, forming a tapestry of ambition and uncertainty. The air was thick with the scent of worn leather and fresh ink, a reminder of the countless contracts signed and dreams forged within these towering structures.

The avenues echoed with the hurried footsteps of brokers and bankers, each step a rhythmic beat in the symphony of commerce. Their faces were a mosaic of determination and fatigue, eyes darting between opportunity and risk, ever calculating, ever hopeful. The city, with its towering glass giants, seemed to pulse with an energy that was both invigorating and oppressive.

Amongst these bustling streets, decisions were forged in the crucible of necessity. There was a silent understanding that every choice, no matter how insignificant it seemed, could ripple across the surface of one's future, altering its course in ways unimaginable. In the shadows of these financial monoliths, the weight of paths taken and lost loomed large, whispering tales of fortunes gained and opportunities missed.

The corridors of power were lined with those who had risen through the ranks, their stories etched into the very fabric of the buildings they inhabited. Each office was a sanctuary of strategy, where the air buzzed with the hum of computers and the rustle of papers, as deals were brokered and alliances formed. Yet, behind the polished veneer of success, there lay the ghosts of choices past, specters of paths not taken, haunting the dreams of those who dared to imagine.

In the quiet moments, when the din of the day subsided, reflections surfaced like echoes from a distant past. The roads not traveled lingered in the mind, a bittersweet reminder of what might have been. They spoke of risks not embraced, of ventures not pursued, and of a different kind of wealth—one measured not in currency but in the richness of experience and the depth of understanding.

As the city lights flickered to life, casting a warm glow over the bustling avenues, a new chapter began to unfold. The choices made today would pave the way for tomorrow's successes or failures, a delicate balance of foresight and fortitude. It was a dance of chance and certainty, where each step could lead to triumph or disaster, and where the only constant was the relentless march of time.

In this world of financial shadows, the paths taken and lost were not merely a series of decisions, but a testament to the resilience of the human spirit. They reflected the courage to venture into the unknown, to navigate the complexities of ambition and desire, and to find meaning amidst the chaos. For in the end, it was not the destination that defined them, but the journey itself, a tapestry woven from the threads of dreams and the echoes of choices past.

# Chapter 12: The Echo of Consequences

## *The Ripple Effect*

In the dim glow of the streetlights, the city pulsed with a life of its own, a sprawling organism fueled by the ceaseless flow of currency. Invisible threads of finance wove through every corner, from the bustling streets of the financial district to the quiet neighborhoods where the hum of daily life continued unabated. The air was thick with the scent of ambition and apprehension, a heady mix that drove the relentless pursuit of prosperity.

Beneath the surface, however, lay a complex tapestry of financial shadows, where every decision, every transaction, sent ripples cascading through the intricate web of economic connections. Here, in this unseen world, the impact of a single choice could be magnified, resonating far beyond its origin and altering the course of countless lives.

At the heart of this dynamic was the stock market, a mercurial entity that shifted and swayed like a living being. Traders, analysts, and investors congregated in its orbit, each one contributing to the ebb and flow of capital. Their actions were like stones cast into a pond, creating waves that spread across the surface, touching everything in their path. A well-timed investment could spark a tide of growth and opportunity, while a misstep could unleash a flood of uncertainty and despair.

Yet, it was not only the titans of industry who wielded such influence. In the quiet of suburban homes, families gathered around kitchen tables, poring over bank statements and budget plans. Their choices, seemingly small and personal, were threads in the larger fabric of the economy. A decision to save or spend, to invest or hold back, could ripple outward, affecting markets and communities in ways both profound and unforeseen.

Consider the local bakery, nestled on a corner of a busy street. Its success depended not only on the quality of its bread but on the myriad financial decisions made by its patrons. A prosperous season for the bakery meant increased orders from suppliers, more hours for employees, and perhaps even an expansion into new markets. Conversely, a downturn could force cutbacks, sending ripples of hardship through the community.

In the boardrooms of towering skyscrapers, executives debated strategies that would shape industries and influence global trade. Their decisions, driven by data and projections, were calculated risks, each one bearing the potential to alter the economic landscape. The ripple effect of their choices extended beyond the confines of their offices, touching lives in distant corners of the world.

Even governments, with their policies and regulations, played a crucial role in this intricate dance. A change in interest rates or a shift in fiscal policy could set off waves of economic activity, affecting everything from employment rates to international relations. The balance of power and prosperity hung in a delicate equilibrium, swayed by the unseen forces of financial shadows.

In this world, nothing existed in isolation. Every action, every decision, was interconnected, part of a vast and ever-evolving network of cause and effect. The ripple effect was a testament to the power and fragility of the economic system, a reminder that in the realm of finance, even the smallest pebble could create waves that reverberated across the globe.

## The Shadows Cast

As the sun dips below the horizon, a stillness envelops the financial district, transforming the bustling metropolis into a landscape of dimly lit avenues and towering silhouettes. The city's glass giants, once gleaming beacons of commerce under the day's light, now stand as quiet sentinels, their reflections melding with the shadows that stretch across the streets like dark tendrils.

In this twilight, the financial world reveals another side, one less visible but no less powerful. The shadows cast by the towering office blocks are mirrored by the unseen forces that lurk within the intricate web of global finance. Here, in the interplay of light and shadow, the complexities of financial markets are both obscured and illuminated.

The streets are lined with echoes of the day's frenetic activity. The hurried footsteps of traders, the urgent whispers of analysts, and the decisive clicks of keyboards have faded into the night, leaving behind an eerie calm. Yet, beneath this calm, the financial machinery hums on, its gears turning silently in the background. The unyielding rhythm of electronic transactions pulses through the veins of the city, an invisible current connecting continents, economies, and lives.

In the dim glow of streetlights, the facades of financial institutions loom with an imposing presence. Their architectural grandeur is both a testament to human ambition and a reminder of the shadows they cast—those intangible, often inscrutable forces that shape economic destinies. These structures, with their cold, reflective surfaces, seem to absorb the night, standing as metaphors for the opacity that often shrouds financial dealings.

Here, in the heart of the financial district, the shadows take on a life of their own. They dance along the edges of awareness, hinting at the unseen risks and opportunities that lie in wait. The shadows are not merely the absence of light but a complex interplay of obscurity and revelation. They represent the hidden variables, the unpredictable market forces, and the human elements that defy quantification.

The night air carries a chill, a reminder that the financial world is not immune to the vagaries of uncertainty. Just as the shadows shift with the movement of the moon, so too does the landscape of finance change with the tides of global events. The shadows whisper of volatility, of fortunes lost and gained in the blink of an eye, and of the ceaseless quest for advantage in a world where nothing is ever truly certain.

Yet, within these shadows lies potential. The darkness conceals not only risks but also the seeds of innovation and growth. For those who dare to venture into the unknown, the shadows offer a canvas upon which new strategies can be painted, new paths forged. It is here, in the interplay of light and shadow, that the future of finance is written—a future shaped by those who understand that the shadows are not to be feared but embraced as part of the landscape.

As the night deepens, the financial district rests in its cloak of shadows, waiting for the first light of dawn to reveal what the darkness has concealed. In this quiet interlude, the shadows cast are both a reflection and a promise of the complexities inherent in the world of finance, a world forever poised on the edge of light and dark.

## Reflections on the Past

In the hushed corridors of memory, the echoes of bygone days linger like whispered secrets. Each step through this labyrinth of recollection reveals the intricate tapestry of choices, failures, and triumphs that have shaped the present. The world of finance, with its dizzying heights and shadowy undercurrents, is a realm where past decisions cast long shadows, influencing the course of future events.

In the dim glow of nostalgia, one can almost see the flickering images of bustling trading floors, where the cacophony of voices and the staccato rhythm of tickers once painted a vibrant picture of ambition and opportunity. The air, thick with anticipation, was charged with the electric promise of prosperity. Yet, beneath this veneer of optimism lay the unspoken fear of loss, a specter that haunted even the boldest of investors.

As the mind drifts further back, scenes from the early days of financial exploration emerge. The pioneers of this world, armed with nothing but intuition and rudimentary tools, ventured into uncharted territories. Their journals, filled with scribbled calculations and hastily drawn graphs, tell tales of daring risks and remarkable resilience. Every decision, whether a masterstroke or a misstep, was a lesson etched into the annals of experience.

These reflections also bring to light the stark realities faced by those who dared to challenge the status quo. The Great Crashes, like ominous milestones, mark the timeline of financial history. In these moments of upheaval, the fragility of human ambition was laid bare, as fortunes crumbled and dreams were dashed against the unforgiving rocks of reality. Yet, from the ashes of despair, new strategies emerged, forged in the crucible of adversity.

The whispers of the past also carry tales of innovation and transformation. The advent of technology, with its relentless march forward, has reshaped the financial landscape in ways once deemed unimaginable. The clatter of typewriters has given way to the silent hum of servers, and the tactile exchange of paper has been replaced by the ephemeral dance of digital transactions. Yet, amidst this whirlwind of progress, the core principles of trust, integrity, and foresight remain steadfast, guiding the hands of those who navigate this complex world.

In these quiet moments of reflection, the stories of individuals who left indelible marks upon the financial realm come to life. Their legacies, woven into the fabric of history, serve as both cautionary tales and sources of inspiration. The visionary who saw beyond the horizon, the strategist who turned the tide of misfortune, the dreamer who dared to defy convention— each has contributed to the evolving narrative of finance.

As the past unfurls its stories, it becomes evident that the shadows it casts are not merely reminders of what once was, but also guiding beacons for what might yet be. The lessons learned, the wisdom gained, and the resilience honed in the fires of experience are the true treasures unearthed from the depths of reflection. In this dance between memory and foresight, the past continues to illuminate the path forward, casting its shadow over the ever-unfolding story of finance.

## The Resonance of Actions

A soft, almost imperceptible hum lingered in the air, as if the very fabric of the room vibrated with the echoes of decisions long past. It was a soundless symphony, one that played in the minds of those who dared to tread the intricate dance of finance, weaving through the shadows that cloaked their intentions. Each choice, each transaction, reverberated, leaving an imprint on the world, like a pebble dropped into a tranquil lake.

The office, a labyrinth of glass and steel, stood as a monument to this unseen orchestra. Sunlight filtered through the windows, casting angular shadows that stretched across the floor, their forms shifting subtly as time slipped by. Within these walls, the air was thick with anticipation, a silent testament to the weight of decisions yet to be made.

At the heart of this dynamic ecosystem, individuals moved with precision and purpose. Their faces, a tapestry of concentration and determination, bore the marks of countless hours spent navigating the labyrinthine corridors of financial strategy. Each figure was a conductor, wielding influence with deft movements, their actions setting into motion a cascade of events that rippled outward, far beyond the confines of their immediate surroundings.

Every choice was a note in the grand composition, harmonizing with others to create a narrative of consequence. The resonance of these actions was felt not just in the rising and falling graphs of stock markets but in the lives of countless individuals whose futures were intertwined with the ebb and flow of financial currents. It was a delicate balance, a dance on the edge of chaos, where the slightest misstep could send shockwaves through the world.

Yet, amidst the calculated chaos, there was an undeniable beauty. The interplay of risk and reward, of ambition and caution, created a rhythm that was both exhilarating and terrifying. It was a reminder that in the realm of finance, nothing existed in isolation. Every decision was a thread in a vast tapestry, woven together by the hands of those who dared to shape the future.

As the day wore on, the hum of activity continued unabated, a testament to the relentless drive of those who thrived in this environment. They understood the power of their actions, the potential for both creation and destruction, and the responsibility that came with wielding such influence. In their hands lay the potential to build empires or to unravel them, to uplift communities or to plunge them into uncertainty.

In the end, the resonance of actions was not just a reflection of individual ambition but a symphony of humanity's collective aspirations and fears. It was a reminder that in the shadows of finance, where decisions were made and futures forged, the echoes of each action would continue to reverberate, shaping the world in ways both seen and unseen. The resonance, though invisible, was undeniable, a testament to the enduring impact of every choice made within those hallowed walls.

# Chapter 13: Embracing the Shadows

## *Accepting the Unknown*

The realm of finance is often depicted as a landscape of certainty and precision, yet beneath its polished veneer lies an intricate web of unpredictability. This very unpredictability is the shadow that looms over every decision, every investment, and every strategy. To the uninitiated, it may appear as a daunting specter, an ominous presence that threatens to unravel the carefully woven tapestry of fiscal plans. However, within this shadow lies an untapped reservoir of potential and opportunity.

The financial world, like the natural world, is governed by a plethora of variables—some known, many unknown. These unknowns are not mere obstacles to be avoided but essential elements that shape the very fabric of the financial landscape. They are the catalysts for innovation, the sparks that ignite the fires of creativity and adaptation. The unknowns force us to question, explore, and venture beyond the confines of the familiar.

In the quiet corridors of financial institutions, where numbers dance across screens and strategies are meticulously crafted, the unknown is a silent companion. It whispers of possibilities not yet realized and challenges the status quo. For those who dare to listen, it offers insights that transcend traditional paradigms, urging a reevaluation of what is deemed possible within the confines of fiscal constraints.

Acceptance of the unknown is not an admission of defeat, but rather a recognition of the dynamic nature of finance. It is an acknowledgment that the path to success is rarely linear and often paved with unexpected detours. Each unforeseen event, each unanticipated market shift, serves as a reminder that the financial world is in a constant state of flux. This fluidity is not a barrier but a bridge—connecting the present with the future, the known with the unknown.

Within the shadows of uncertainty lies a profound opportunity for growth and transformation. It is here, in the ambiguity, that innovation thrives. The unknown invites a departure from conventional thinking, encouraging the development of new strategies that are resilient and adaptable. It demands a mindset that is agile, one that can pivot and adjust in response to emerging trends and unforeseen challenges.

The art of accepting the unknown is akin to navigating a vast ocean with no fixed destination. It requires a willingness to set sail without the assurance of calm seas or favorable winds. Yet, it is precisely this willingness that unlocks the potential for discovery and advancement. In the financial world, those who embrace the unknown are often those who chart new territories, uncovering hidden opportunities and redefining the boundaries of what is achievable.

In the end, the unknown is not something to be feared but embraced as an integral component of the financial journey. It is the shadow that accompanies every decision, casting its influence over every choice. To accept the unknown is to acknowledge its power, to harness its potential, and to transform its ambiguity into a source of strength and innovation. It is this acceptance that ultimately defines the pioneers of finance, those who lead not with certainty but with courage, navigating the shadows with an unwavering resolve.

## Finding Balance

The delicate dance between financial ambition and personal fulfillment is akin to walking a tightrope suspended in the vast expanse of life's demands. Every step taken requires a calculated precision, an acute awareness of the forces at play, and a steadfast resolve to maintain equilibrium amidst the swirling winds of opportunity and obligation. This balance, elusive yet essential, is the cornerstone of navigating the financial shadows that loom over one's aspirations.

In the heart of a bustling city, where skyscrapers punctuate the skyline like ambitious dreams etched against the canvas of the sky, individuals weave through the tapestry of urban life, each carrying their own hopes and burdens. The city hums with the rhythm of commerce, a symphony of transactions that orchestrate the flow of capital and ambition. Yet, beneath this vibrant exterior lies the quiet struggle of finding harmony between the pursuit of wealth and the nourishment of the soul.

Within the walls of high-rise offices, the clatter of keyboards and the murmur of voices form a backdrop to the relentless quest for financial success. Here, the allure of prosperity beckons with promises of security and status, a siren song that tempts many to lose sight of other vital facets of life. Yet, beneath the surface, there lingers a subtle awareness that true wealth extends beyond monetary accumulation.

Amidst the cacophony of fiscal ambitions, there exists a yearning for moments of stillness, where one can pause and reflect on the values that truly matter. It is in these moments of introspection that the realization dawns: the pursuit of financial gain must be tempered with a commitment to personal well-being and the cultivation of meaningful relationships. The heart seeks solace in the warmth of human connection, in the laughter shared with loved ones, and in the serene embrace of nature's beauty.

As the sun sets, casting a golden glow over the cityscape, a sense of tranquility descends upon the world. It is in this twilight hour that the intricate balance becomes visible, a delicate interplay of light and shadow that mirrors the duality of financial pursuits and personal fulfillment. The shadows, once perceived as ominous, now reveal themselves as integral elements of a larger, harmonious picture.

To navigate the financial shadows is to acknowledge the multifaceted nature of wealth, recognizing that true prosperity encompasses both material success and the richness of a life well-lived. It requires a conscious effort to prioritize time and energy, invest in experiences that nurture the soul, and cultivate a mindset that values balance over excess.

The journey towards finding balance is not a linear path, but a dynamic process of continuous adjustment and refinement. It demands resilience and the courage to question societal norms that equate financial achievement with happiness. In embracing this journey, one discovers that the shadows, far from being obstacles, can serve as guides on the path to a more fulfilling existence.

In the quiet moments, when the world slows and the mind finds clarity, the realization emerges that balance is not a destination but a state of being. It is a commitment to living with intention, to making choices that honor both ambition and contentment, and to embracing the shadows as integral parts of the journey towards a life of true abundance.

## *The Dance of Light and Shadow*

In the dim glow of the evening, the cityscape transforms into a canvas, where lights flicker like stars fallen from the heavens, weaving a tapestry of brilliance and mystery. The financial district, once bustling with the rhythmic cadence of footsteps and the hum of ambition, now stands in a delicate balance between illumination and obscurity.

Skyscrapers, those towering sentinels of commerce, pierce the night sky, their windows shimmering with the reflection of streetlights and neon signs. Each pane of glass becomes a portal, revealing glimpses of the world within, where shadows stretch and contract, playing a silent symphony against the backdrop of opulence and austerity.

In this urban expanse, shadows whisper tales of fortunes made and lost, of dreams nurtured and shattered. They dance across the polished marble floors of grand lobbies, where echoes of hurried conversations and clinking glasses linger like ghosts of transactions past. The shadows, like silent witnesses, observe the ebb and flow of wealth, casting long fingers that touch upon the aspirations and anxieties of those who walk beneath them.

The interplay of light and shadow is nowhere more pronounced than in the glass-walled boardrooms perched high above the city streets. Here, decisions are made, strategies crafted, and destinies forged. The light, sharp and unyielding, cuts through the gloom, illuminating the faces of those gathered, yet leaving parts of the room shrouded in mystery. It is in these spaces that the true nature of the financial world is revealed—a world where clarity and opacity coexist, each vying for dominance.

In the quieter corners, where the light is softer and shadows more forgiving, the stories of those who toil behind the scenes unfold. The custodians of the financial realm, with their meticulous records and keen eyes, work diligently, their efforts often hidden in the creases of darkness that hug the edges of their domain. Here, the dance is more subdued, yet no less significant, as the balance between light and shadow dictates the rhythm of their labor.

Outside, as the night deepens, the city pulses with an energy all its own. The glow from shopfronts spills onto the pavement, mingling with the shadows cast by towering edifices. In this interplay, the financial shadows take on a life of their own, weaving stories that stretch beyond the confines of walls and windows. They slip through alleyways, curl around corners, and climb facades, a silent testament to the ceaseless motion of the city's heartbeat.

Yet, amidst this dance, there exists a fragile equilibrium. The light, with its promise of transparency and revelation, strives to banish the shadows, to expose what lies hidden. The shadows, in turn, cling to their secrets, offering solace and protection to those who seek refuge from the relentless scrutiny of the world above.

Thus, the dance of light and shadow continues, an eternal waltz that shapes the very essence of the financial realm. It is a dance that defines the boundaries of what is seen and what remains unseen, a delicate choreography that ensures the city, and all who dwell within it, continue to thrive amidst the ever-shifting tides of fortune and fate.

## A New Perspective

As the sun cast its golden hue over the bustling financial district, the city seemed to hum with a rhythm all its own. Skyscrapers stood like sentinels, their glass facades reflecting the vibrant energy of the metropolis, while the streets below teemed with people, each one carrying their own hopes and dreams. Amidst the chaos, a sense of transformation lingered in the air, an undercurrent of change that was almost palpable.

In this ever-evolving landscape, a new perspective was quietly taking shape. It was not born of radical shifts or dramatic upheavals but rather emerged from the subtle interplay of old and new. The financial world, long governed by tradition and convention, was beginning to embrace innovation, albeit cautiously. This change was not immediately visible to the untrained eye, but for those who knew where to look, it was unmistakable.

The heart of this transformation lay in the adoption of technology, an invisible hand guiding the market's pulse. Algorithms danced through networks, executing trades with a precision that human hands could never achieve. Data flowed like a river, a ceaseless stream of information that painted a picture of the world's economy in real-time. The age of digital finance was dawning, and with it came an opportunity to redefine what was possible.

Amidst this digital renaissance, the human element remained as crucial as ever. The seasoned traders, with their wealth of experience and intuition, found themselves working alongside a new generation of analysts who spoke the language of code and computation. Together, they forged a path through the complexities of the market, each bringing their unique strengths to the table.

There was a certain beauty in this collaboration, a harmonious blending of the old and the new. It was as if the financial world had discovered a new lens through which to view itself, one that revealed possibilities previously hidden from sight. This shift in perspective extended beyond the trading floors and boardrooms, touching every aspect of the industry.

Investors, too, began to see the world through fresh eyes. No longer content with the status quo, they sought out opportunities that aligned with their values, considering not just potential profits but also the impact of their investments on the planet and its people. Environmental, social, and governance factors became integral to decision-making, a testament to the growing awareness of the interconnectedness of global systems.

In this era of change, adaptability became the watchword. Those who thrived were the ones who embraced this new perspective, viewing challenges not as obstacles but as opportunities for growth. The world of finance was no longer a static entity but a dynamic ecosystem, constantly in flux yet full of promise.

As the day drew to a close and the city lights began to twinkle against the darkening sky, one could not help but feel a sense of anticipation. The future, once shrouded in uncertainty, now seemed to beckon with the promise of endless possibilities. The financial shadows that had long loomed over the industry were beginning to recede, revealing a landscape rich with potential and ripe for exploration.